WITHDRAWN

DECIDING TO BE LEGAL

DECIDING

TO BE LEGAL

A MAYA COMMUNITY IN HOUSTON

Jacqueline Maria Hagan

Temple University Press ～ Philadelphia

Temple University Press, Philadelphia 19122

Copyright © 1994 by Temple University

All rights reserved

Published 1994

Printed in the United States of America

The paper used in this publication meets the minimum requirements of American National Standard for Information Sciences—Permanence of Paper for Printed Library Materials,

ANSI Z39.48-1984 ∞

LIBRARY OF CONGRESS CATALOGING-IN-PUBLICATION DATA

Hagan, Jacqueline Maria, 1954—
    Deciding to be legal: a Maya community in Houston / Jacqueline
Maria Hagan.
        p.   cm.
    Includes bibliographical references and index.
    ISBN 1-56639-256-x (cl. : alk. paper). — ISBN 1-56639-257-8 (pbk. :
alk. paper)
    1. Mayas—Urban residence—Texas—Houston. 2. Mayas—Legal
status, laws, etc.—Texas—Houston. 3. Mayas—Texas—
Houston—Social conditions. 4. Immigrants—Texas—Houston.
5. Totonicapán (Guatemala : Dept.)—Emigration and
immigration. 6. Houston (Tex.)—Emigration and
immigration. 7. United States—Emigration and immigration—
Government policy. 8. United States. Immigration Reform and
Control Act of 1986.   I. Title.
E99.M433H34 1994
305.897'407641411—dc20   94 39636
                                                    CIP

To my father and mother,
whose influence has made a cross-cultural perspective
both a personal goal and an academic pursuit.

CONTENTS

TABLES

PREFACE AND
ACKNOWLEDGMENTS

THE MAYA IMMIGRANTS AMONG WHOM I LIVED IN HOUSton repeatedly talked about the cultural uneasiness they felt in moving from their Guatemalan highland villages to their Houston apartment dwellings. Their reactions touched a very personal chord, for the cultural marginality they described as strangers in a new land sounded much like my own experiences. Moving across national borders has been a regular feature of my life. My parents were of different nationalities and, as the daughter of a career diplomat, I became accustomed to frequent changes of residence including eight different countries before I finished high school. When my father retired from the U.S. foreign service in the early 1970s, the family settled in my mother's homeland, Costa Rica. Soon afterward, I joined them and spent several years teaching at a local elementary school and polishing my rusty Spanish. In the mid-eighties I returned to the United States to pursue an academic career in sociology and demography.

My interest in the migration process and my strong ties to Central America led me to select Central American migration as my major field of research. Originally, my idea was to return to Costa Rica and do an ethnography of resettlement among refugee families in the country. Fearing I might "go native," my mentor and dear friend Harley Browning encouraged me to focus on Central American settlement in the United States. To facilitate this change in research direction, Harley introduced me to a recent graduate of the University of Texas, Nestor Rodríguez, who was in the beginning stages of what would become a Ford Foundation–sponsored project focusing on intergroup relations between undocumented new-comer immigrants and established resident groups in Houston, Texas.

Field researchers have written about the methodological problems of studying the undocumented, especially the problem of gaining research access to this clandestine population (Chavez 1992; 1988; Cornelius, 1982). Fortunately, I was spared this difficulty. Nestor introduced me to key members of a Guatemalan Maya community in Houston, and with time my interest in studying their settlement experiences grew. In the summer of 1986, several months before the Immigration Reform and Control Act (IRCA) was passed into law, I began a weekly commute to Houston to do research among the Maya. The following summer, I moved to Houston and located an apartment in one of the several large complexes that house the majority of the Totonicapán Maya community. I lived among these people for three years, through the spring of 1990, a period covering the span of the legalization program, and spent one summer in their home community in the western highland Department (province) of Totonicapán, Guatemala.

While gathering data for my dissertation, I was funded by Nestor's Ford Foundation grant and by Robert L. Bach, at SUNY–Binghamton, who was conducting a U.S. Labor Department–sponsored study of the effects of IRCA on local labor markets. Working on these two large projects allowed me to place my study of Maya settlement in Houston within the context of national immigration policy reform, thus providing both macro and micro perspectives on the issue of migrant settlement.

The process of establishing trust among the Totonicapán Maya was accelerated by my increasing visibility in the community. At the invitation of key informants, I began attending community events, such as baptisms, birthdays, *quinceañeras* (a coming-out celebration for fifteen-year-old girls), weddings, and soccer games. With time I became a familiar face in the housing complex, and the residents began to accept my presence. And as their trust increased, so did their willingness to approach me for assistance and to share with me their daily lives. Reciprocity emerged as an essential ingredient in the success of the field research. In sharing a meal with a family, accompanying a migrant to a job interview, or registering a child in school, I gathered the richest data on their settlement experience.

In the end, I was accepted into the homes and lives of the Maya through the multiple roles I assumed. I was more than a researcher. I was a friend, counselor, mediator, and fellow tenant and, as such, I gained the insights that came with these roles. With time I became known as the in-house translator for the Spanish-speaking tenants and served as cultural broker between the Maya community and the host society. In these roles, I translated correspondence, arranged appointments with doctors, and helped immigrants prepare their documents for legalization. To become proficient in the technical and legal aspects of the legalization process I worked at a local Qualified Designated Entity (QDE) involved in organizing and filing immigrant legalization applications. Helping with legalization enabled me to gather information pertinent to individual, group, and community legalization experiences. Living within the community and assuming these multiple roles allowed me to track changes in immigrants' attitudes and behaviors as they related to the legalization program (e.g., motivations for applying, decision making, community strategies ensuring participation, and experiences with the local INS [Immigration and Naturalization Service] office).

Three years of fieldwork generated longitudinal data both on community-level behavioral patterns and on the individual experiences of seventy-four key informants. Community-

level data were collected primarily through participant observation. Living in the Maya neighborhood enabled me to
observe their settlement behavior as residents of the area.
Attending community events in Houston and in Guatemala
enabled me to keep track of immigrants' social and cultural
activities and to identify the many networks which, linked
together, constituted the Maya community structure. Traveling to Guatemala with a group of newly legalized immigrants
enabled me to observe the effects of legalization on the home
community and on social ties between the two communities.

The bulk of the individual-level data emerged during long
conversations with immigrants in my apartment, during job
interviews to which I accompanied many of the female domestic workers, and during the process of assisting immigrants with the legalization applications. I kept a longitudinal
data-base file and a memo file on each of the seventy-four
Maya in my sample. The data-base file included three basic
categories of information: immigration, sociodemographic,
and labor market. Immigration data included information on
community of origin, time of arrival, legal status, and return
migration. Sociodemographic data included information on
gender, age, marital status, education, and household composition. Labor market information consisted of job type, earnings, number of jobs held, industrial sector, ethnicity of
employer/supervisor, ethnicity of coworkers and labor market
type. These data were recorded over the three-year period.

Individual memo files were developed primarily from conversations with individuals and included unsolicited accounts
relating to migration (e.g., the immigrant's reasons for migrating to Houston), community relations (e.g., community
events in which the immigrant regularly participated), settlement patterns (e.g., the immigrant's residential mobility while
in Houston), and legalization (e.g., issues influencing the
immigrant's decision to apply for legalization, sources of documentation, and experiences with the INS).

To illustrate how this process of data collection evolved, I elaborate on the research relationship and personal friendship I developed with Soledad, a young Maya woman and recent migrant to Houston. I first met Soledad in October of 1987 when she stopped by my apartment with Marta, another Maya I had met some months before. Soledad had just given birth to her first child and was planning to send her newborn daughter to Guatemala to live with her mother so that she could work full-time in Houston. I told Soledad about my study and expressed interest in what, at the time, appeared to be an unusual case. (In fact, I was to come across many such cases in which a U.S. born child was sent back to Guatemala so that the migrant mother could begin or resume full time employment in Houston and the child could be exposed to the Maya culture back home.) After discussing the case with me, Soledad agreed to be part of my study so long as her name was not revealed. I encouraged her to come visit me at her convenience and offered to help in any way I could. Some weeks later, Soledad returned—this time alone—and told me that her child had left for Guatemala with a friend and that she would appreciate my help in finding a position as a live-in domestic. At the time I had no leads, but I promised to let her know as soon as something came up. During this same visit, I gathered all the basic immigration and sociodemographic data on Soledad and asked her to keep in touch. Several weeks later I was called by a potential employer who was looking for a domestic. (By this time my name was well known among several employer networks that had hired other Maya women in the community.) I arranged an interview between Soledad and the employer and accompanied Soledad on the day of her interview. In so doing I was able to examine the process of hiring a recent arrival and to gather considerable information on the employer. After Soledad was hired, we continued to keep in touch for the remaining two years of the study. When it came time for Soledad to apply for legalization, I returned to her employer to obtain an affidavit of her employment history to submit with Soledad's application. Like many other employers of such domestics, however, Soledad's employer was unwilling to supply the documentation and, consequently, Soledad was unable to acquire legal status.

Soledad was one of the many women in the community with whom I developed very close ties. My close relationship with these women is evidenced by the fact that more of my data were gathered from women and about women than from or about men. This discrepancy can partially be explained by the traditional norms governing relations between women and men in this particular community. A pattern developed in which most men—if given the choice—would seek Nestor's assistance, while most of the women would seek mine. Even though I had several key informants among the men, and relied on them substantially, and although I was also able to solicit considerable information via Nestor's interviews, my study does place greater emphasis on the settlement experiences of women. The theme of men's and women's different settlement experiences emerged early in the research process and runs through the entire book.

As Soledad's case illustrates, I adopted a reflexive and conversational approach to the interviewing schedule. I wanted the immigrants to feel at ease so that their world of meaning would emerge from their own personal experiences rather than from the design of the research instrument itself. At no time did I tape these conversations, although I did keep a daily journal of observations and interviews. The precarious state of being undocumented, and the sensitivity of the legalization issue, called for such an approach to gathering data.

Data analysis was quite simple and straight forward. I began by identifying categories by which to organize my recorded observations and interviews. In addition to maintaining the individual data files, I organized my data into descriptive categories, such as jobs, neighborhoods, gender, legalization, and community events. Classifying the data into various topics was determined, in part, by my original research interests and, in part, by the observations made in the field. During the course of the research, the categories underwent considerable change as they shifted from the more descriptive to the more analytical. Thus, for example, the legalization category eventually was refined and expanded to account for the social processes of legalization (e.g., motivations to apply, decision making, social networks and program participation, legal status, and migration patterns).

The principal reason for using the ethnographic method was that such an approach enabled me to observe, in detail and over time, the complex web of social interaction between two processes: the settlement of an immigrant community and the local implementation of immigration policy reform. With this approach one is permitted to examine social action in a more complete form—as it unfolds and as it is understood by the actors themselves. I sought to understand the meaning that the immigrants attached to legalization, to capture the lives of the immigrants as they experienced legalization, and to examine how legalization influenced their settlement behavior.

An ethnographic case-study approach also offered several practical advantages for understanding the settlement behavior of an undocumented Maya community. Some of these advantages are obvious and are well known in undocumented immigration studies. First, because we do not know the precise size or geographic location of the undocumented population in the United States, it is impossible to use other data-collection techniques (e.g., surveys) since they typically rely on a random sampling procedure. This same problem applies to the newcomer Maya population, whose numbers are small and visibility low compared with other Central Americans in the United States. A second reason for deciding on an ethnographic approach relates to the surreptitious nature of undocumented settlement. The undocumented typically lead clandestine lives, fearing the consequences of detection by INS authorities. Thus, they are not very open to activities, such as being interviewed, that might draw attention to their presence. Their precarious legal status called for a nonintrusive approach that ethnography is best suited to accommodate.

I AM GRATEFUL TO THE COMMUNITIES, families, institutions, and many individuals who have contributed to this study. I am indebted to the Maya immigrants in Houston who shared their time, their day-to-day experiences, and their personal migration and legalization histories. They welcomed me into their lives and homes and taught me the joys and hardships of immigrant life.

The emotional support I have received from my own family can not be measured. My father, John Hagan, encouraged educational aspirations in his six children without making distinctions between sons and daughters; my desire to learn and to teach is rooted in the values he instilled in me. To my mother, Maria Teresa Hagan, I owe a debt of gratitude for believing in her children and opening our minds to the many cultures of the world. I also want to thank my brother, Sean, and my sisters, Pisha, Moni, Tara, and Terry, for being my best friends and providing me with unconditional support during the life of this project.

Among the many individuals who deserve recognition, Harley Browning merits special thanks. It would be difficult to acknowledge the debt I owe Harley for the patient and consistent support he extended to me throughout my graduate career and the writing of this book. Harley pushed me beyond what I had believed were my capabilities and, in doing so, proved himself a great mentor and friend.

I would also like to thank Bryan Roberts who helped to

hone my skills as a field researcher and helped to refine my ideas and insights into analytical categories. Richard Adams also deserves special mention for providing invaluable insight into the Maya culture as well as active participation in many stages of this study. Theresa Sullivan has been a constant in my professional development and has offered valuable feedback on all stages of the research. I would also like to thank Frank Bean who provided useful comments on an early draft of this book.

Writing this book would have been extremely difficult without the assistance and support of others. Special thanks goes to my friend and colleague, Janet Chafetz, whose intellectual generosity and editing skills fine tuned many of my ideas and certainly polished the overall style of this book. A very warm thanks goes to Susan González Baker who, not only offered unparalleled friendship but also helped me locate my research in the larger context of immigration policy reform. I would also like to thank Audrey Singer, James Loucky, and the anonymous reviewers for their useful comments and suggestions.

My appreciation is also extended to my editor, Doris Braendel, whose enthusiastic support and concrete advice pushed the book to completion, and to the copyeditors at Martin-Waterman Associates, Judith Waterman and Charles Purrenhage, for further clarifying my arguments. Several students at the University of Houston also merit recognition for the research assistance they provided during the final months of writing—Melissa Kubala, Kelly Troup, Mimi Hinnawi, Mark Hinnawi, Andrew Krieger, Susana McCollom, Hwonchu Kwon, and Jennifer Varela.

Several institutions supported me as well. The Population Research Center at the University of Texas–Austin provided the intellectual atmosphere in which to develop the research ideas on which this book is based. A grant from the Ford Foundation provided Nestor Rodríguez and me with the financial support to complete more than two years of ethnographic investigation among migrant communities in Houston. Funding from the Institute on International Labor and Multiculturalism at SUNY–Binghamton also facilitated this study; special thanks go to Robert L. Bach, who made this funding possible, encouraged my research, and challenged my ideas and arguments. Since my arrival in Houston, the University of Houston has provided me with resources to complete this book. I thank all of the faculty and departmental staff, especially A. Gary Dworkin, Helen-Rose Ebaugh, Mary J. Duncan, and Lonnie Anderson for their assistance and support. I also owe a debt of gratitude to local community organizations and several attorneys who shared their stories and expertise.

Most important, I want to thank my research partner and dear friend, Nestor Rodríguez. Not only did Nestor introduce me to the Maya community, he also showed me the ropes of doing ethnography. Through Nestor I learned the importance of generosity and restraint in conducting field research. He was always on hand to discuss and clarify my field observations, while never imposing his own ideas. Working with Nestor has been one of the most satisfying aspects of this work. In many ways this is *our* study.

PART ONE

BUILDING A COMMUNITY STRUCTURE IN HOUSTON

CHAPTER ONE

INTRODUCTION

ONE COLD, WINTER DAWN IN 1978, YOUNG JUAN XUC, A subsistence farmer and weaver, said good-bye to his wife and his two children and walked alone down a dirt road, taking the first steps of his journey from the western highlands of Guatemala to Houston, Texas. More than one thousand other Maya from his hometown of San Pedro were to follow his footsteps into the next decade.

The motivation that took Juan by foot and bus over the highlands of Guatemala, through Mexico, and across the Rio Grande into the United States was the need to help his youngest son who was afflicted with cancer. His plan was simple: to find a job in Houston and earn enough money to secure the best medical attention there for his son. His first attempt to cross the Rio Grande was unsuccessful. Several miles from the U.S.–Mexico border, he was apprehended by INS border agents. He identified himself as Mexican, so the agents sent him back across the river. His second attempt was a success. Hiding under the bed of a truck hauling fruit to the Rio Grande Valley area, he crossed the border and then made his way—on foot—to Houston.

When Juan arrived in Houston, he encountered a boomtown. Jobs were everywhere to be had. The escalating price of oil during the 1970s had sent the area's economy into a state of hypergrowth, stimulating a demand for labor, especially low-wage and low-skill, to fill jobs in the support service industries. Within days of his arrival, Juan had secured a job as a maintenance man for an apartment complex owned and operated by an Anglo couple. Juan's earliest impressions of Houston were not (as one might suspect of someone who had never traveled to an industrial urban country) the forms of towering skyscrapers or the multitude of electronic gadgets and other consumer goods in the store windows, but the nontraditional gender roles of the couple for whom he worked:

> He cleaned the house and cooked the food, and she watched television and drank beer. I had never seen a woman drink or a man clean house. When I think of my first Houston memories, I think of the strange way in which this married couple behaved towards one another. I still am unable to understand these cultural differences.

After three months in the city, Juan met another Maya, a man from El Quiché, a department neighboring his native Department of Totonicapán in the Guatemala highlands. Several weeks later, his new friend had found him a better-paying job as a maintenance worker in the retail supermarket chain where he worked. Shortly after landing this job, Juan moved in with eight other undocumented coworkers in a crowded, one-bedroom apartment located in the southwest part of the city.

The first fellow Maya to follow in Juan's steps from San Pedro was Pablo, his brother-in-law, also a weaver and farmer on the family *milpa* (cornfield). Through his new contacts at work, Juan was able to find a maintenance position for Pablo in the supermarket chain. It was not long before news of

The migrant pioneers, Juan and Carmen, visit the grave site of their youngest son in San Pedro.

higher wages and economic opportunity in Houston reached San Pedro. Juan began receiving letters from kin and friends, asking him to find them work in Houston. According to Juan, it was not uncommon for him to receive three or four such letters in a day. The social foundation for Maya migration from San Pedro to Houston had been laid.

By the fall of 1981 Juan had assumed the informal role of supervisor ("El Encargado") of the maintenance crew at the supermarket. He was now earning five dollars an hour and had saved enough money to send for his wife, Carmen, his daughter, María, and his ailing son, Antonito. Antonito was able to spend his last months with his family in Houston before his death in 1982. Juan's remaining savings were spent on an elaborate family sepulcher in San Pedro, Guatemala, where is son now rests.

Supervisors and employers within the supermarket chain

began asking the Maya men if they had sisters or wives who
wanted to work for them as domestics. Since wage employment opportunities for women in San Pedro are mainly limited to occasional domestic work, many of the San Pedro
women were eager to supplement their family's subsistence
farming and join kin in Houston. In the fall of 1981 and
spring of 1982, the first stream of sisters and wives from San
Pedro arrived. They, in turn, began recruiting other women
from San Pedro. Ten years later, many households in San
Pedro had ties with Maya immigrant households in Houston.
Social networks extended out from San Pedro and developed
from adjacent towns and farming settlements in the highlands, including those from San Antonio de Belén, San
Rafael, and Ojo de Agua. All the arriving Maya settled in the
same southwest area of Houston where Juan had settled.

As the size of the Maya population in Houston increased,
Juan's leadership role among the Maya expanded to initiating
community activities, as well as recruiting more workers and,
thus, facilitating his job mobility in Houston and social
mobility in San Pedro. In the mid-eighties, Juan organized
the first of two soccer teams made up of San Pedro migrants.
By 1987, partially as a result of his successful recruitment of a
work crew for the retail supermarket chain, Juan was promoted to the produce section and was earning ten dollars an hour.
As Juan observes, in the process of settling in Houston, many
in the community, while dedicated to maintaining their ethnic identity, also began to realize the American Dream.

> When I got to Houston ten years ago, I knew no one here
> and nothing about the way people live. But I looked, and
> I saw, and I wondered, and I learned. In Houston, if you
> have no friends and have no credit cards, you have
> nothing. The credit cards take the place of friends. They
> open doors for you. They vouch for you. They help you
> get things done. *To have credit is to be American.* At first,
> seeing people use credit cards just made me curious, but

I figured out how much easier they were than using money; it made me want one. I now have several cards. One adapts, one learns. But what we are inside—*indígena* [as the Maya migrants refer to themselves among non-Mayas]—never changes.

We seldom have the opportunity to identify the pioneer of an undocumented community. One of the enormous successes of my initial fieldwork was gaining Juan and Carmen as informants. As their story tells us, Juan and Carmen not only paved the way for the first flow of Maya from the community of San Pedro in the highlands of Guatemala to Houston but also assumed a role as architects of the community's basic social structure in Houston. Juan and Carmen were my entrée to the homes of the more established as well as the more recent members of the community who provided me with their settlement histories. Their stories, along with several years of field observation and community participation, enabled me to trace the development of a Maya community in Houston from its genesis and describe the settlement process of its members. In the course of this work, I sought to identify those features which constitute a well-developed community structure and which might explain the successful adaptation experienced by many of the migrants in the community. In addition, understanding the community structure provides a base from which we can chart community response and change resulting from the 1986 Immigration Reform and Control Act (IRCA).

THIS BOOK TELLS SEVERAL STORIES. It tells the story of Maya migration from rural Guatemala to urban North America.[1] It tells the story of Maya settlement and community development in Houston, Texas. And it tells the story of how one undocumented Maya community interpreted and acted upon major immigration policy reform.

The Maya are the largest, and perhaps most diverse,

indigenous group in North America. More than 4 million Maya, belonging to over twenty linguistic groups, live in Guatemala, Mexico and, most recently, in the United States. Beginning in the mid- to late 1970s, Maya from distinct communities in southern Mexico and the western highlands of Guatemala began the journey north. Fleeing political strife and economic hardship, tens of thousands of Maya sought political safety and economic security in Mexico and the United States (Frelick 1991; Ferris 1987; Torres-Rivas 1985; Aguayo and Weiss-Fagen 1988; Hagan 1986; Aguayo 1985). For some, the journey was a short one, ending in nearby refugee camps in southern Mexico. For others, the journey took them through Mexico and into the United States, where they have since settled and established communities in Houston, Los Angeles, and southern Florida, among other places (Burns 1993; Loucky 1988; Rodríguez 1987).

The Maya who have settled in the United States consider themselves members of specific communities that generally correspond to the smallest administrative division in Guatemala, the *municipio* (township).[2] Municipios represented in the United States are numerous. Small towns in Florida and Arizona as well as neighborhoods in large cities like Houston, Los Angeles, San Francisco, and Chicago are now the settings of the new Maya communities in the United States.

This book is about one such community—the over one thousand or so Maya women, men, and children who made the journey from the municipio of San Pedro, located in the Department of Totonicapán, to Houston, Texas, in search of economic opportunity.[3] Our central concern is the settlement behavior of this undocumented Maya community in the context of changing immigration policy: namely, the implementation of the legalization provision of IRCA, which granted roughly 1.7 million undocumented immigrants legal status. It is also a book about the development and dynamics of a strong Maya community structure in Houston; about the differential settlement experiences of men and women; about the maintenance of social ties with the home community; about how the Maya interpreted and responded to the legalization program; about how settlement plans shifted as a result of legalization.

In the fall of 1986, when IRCA was passed into law, Congress sent the Immigration and Naturalization Service two messages: cut the flow and redefine the stock of undocumented immigrants. To cut the flow, the INS would both implement sanctions for employers who hired illegal aliens and reinforce the border with new officers. Simultaneously, to redefine the stock, the INS would implement a "generous" legalization program for the pre-1982 resident undocumented population (U.S. House of Representatives 1986). Not even IRCA's staunchest critics can deny the success of the legalization program: the numbers speak to its success. It legalized nearly 2 million applicants. In fact, it will probably be recorded as the single most ambitious and successful program in the history of U.S. immigration policy, considering the size and the proportion of the estimated eligible population whose status has been legalized.[4]

Researchers since 1986 have sought primarily to evaluate the consequences of IRCA, especially the effects of the "employer sanctions" provision on the U.S. wage structure (Lowell et al. 1991), undocumented immigrant flows (Bean et al. 1990b), and employment-related discrimination (Cross et al. 1990; U.S. General Accounting Office 1987, 1988, 1990). Ironically, most of these studies find that employer sanctions have had little tangible effect, while the significance of legalization has only recently begun to be explored in either sociological or policy terms (Hagan and Baker 1993). In addition, most post-IRCA research has focused exclusively on Mexican immigration, little attention having been given to a growing component of our immigrant population—Central Americans.

My study departs from most of the post-IRCA research. I am concerned with understanding the legalization provision of IRCA from the perspective of the policy targets—the immigrant communities. I hope to illustrate the active role immigrants assume in interpreting, evaluating, and responding to immigration policy via their community structure. By relying on the points of view of those who are most affected by immigration policy and yet least often heard—immigrant communities—I hope to highlight the importance of women, family, and community considerations in decisions regarding legal status, and I suggest that there exists far more diversity of opportunity and response to legalization than may have been envisioned by its framers. Thus, this ethnography questions popular myths about the settlement of immigrant communities and raises important issues regarding the further development of immigration policies.

Two main issues preoccupied me during the course of researching and writing this book. First was the relationship between migrant community structure and settlement opportunities. Intuitively, one might expect that migrants coming from a rural setting, retaining a traditionally Maya culture, and possessing few transferable job skills would not fare well in a metropolitan milieu such as Houston. Yet, compared with other Central Americans in the city, the Maya from Totonicapán have achieved exceptional adaptation in Houston's modern setting. This paradox can be explained by the strong community structure developed by the Totonicapán Maya in Houston (the subject of Chapters Two and Three). Since their arrival in Houston in the late seventies, the Maya have developed extensive community-based networks while maintaining strong cultural and economic ties with the home community in Guatemala. These well-developed organizational forms not only regulate migratory flows but also explain the successful Maya settlement experience (Rodríguez 1987; Rodríguez and Hagan 1989).

This community feature was an important consideration in selecting a migrant community for study, for I defined a well-developed social structure as a prerequisite for examining community responses to legalization and for identifying community changes stemming from the IRCA program. Of theoretical interest, then, is the extent to which migrant social networks (i.e., personal ties based on family, kin, friendship, and community) assist or hinder adjustment. That is, as most migration scholars argue (Massey et al. 1987; Macdonald and Macdonald 1974), does being a member of various community social networks provide resources upon which community members can draw in the adaptation process, one aspect of which is, in the case of this study, the adjustment to legal status? Or, as others have suggested (Kritz and Gurak 1984; Tilly and Brown 1967), does membership in community networks impede or delay adjustment?

The second main avenue of research emerged naturally out of my initial observations and findings. As the numbers of community members (eligible and ineligible) applying for temporary residency under the legalization program swelled, so did my interest in how legal status would influence two related community processes: settlement behavior and social networks between the sending and receiving communities. That is, would legal status lead to the settlement of a permanent Maya community in Houston? And, if so, how would such a development affect the nature of relations between the two communities? Would legal status engender stronger ties to the host community and thereby weaken, or perhaps even sever, networks between the two communities? This could result as newly legalized immigrants began to identify more with the host community and as community members in Guatemala began to fear the undocumented journey north under the specter of IRCA's employer sanctions provision. Or, would legal status become a new resource in the community, one that would sustain or generate new patterns of migration and settlement? If this was the result, the cultural and economic ties between Houston and villages in the western highlands of Guatemala would be maintained, perhaps be strengthened.

The following chapters fall naturally into two groups. In the first I describe the building of a Maya community in Houston. Within this account, the relationship between community structure and immigrant adaptation and incorporation is emphasized, along with the differing settlement experiences of men and women. The discussion reflects two dimensions of community formation: 1. the transfer and reproduction of cultural resources associated with a common community of origin and a Maya identity—the focus of Chapter Two; and 2. the settlement process, including the residential configuration of the community, the transformation of kinship structure, recruitment networks and the journey, living arrangements, job networks and the work experience, and the formation of a community church and a community soccer club (these features are examined in Chapter Three).

The second group of the chapters takes the reader through the legalization process as viewed and interpreted by the Maya community. In Chapter Four, I trace the social and technical process of acquiring legal residence. Changes in the community that result from legalization are the subject of Chapter Five. In Chapter Six, we go beyond the Maya narrative to the wider implications of this study for migration theory and research and for immigration policy making.

CHAPTER TWO

COMMUNITY OF ORIGIN AND THE TRANSFER OF CULTURAL RESOURCES

UNDOUBTEDLY THE MOST MEANINGFUL SOCIAL TIE THAT BONDS the Maya migrants in Houston is a shared community of origin. Common cultural identity, which is strongly associated with a sense of place in the Guatemalan highlands, promotes a feeling of belonging among the San Pedro Maya in Houston. The transfer of cultural features from the home community to the host community also serves as an important basis for community development in Houston. It will be helpful, therefore, to describe, if briefly, the distinctive features of the community structure they left behind.

⭐ THE COMMUNITY THEY LEFT BEHIND: PLACE, PEOPLE, AND CULTURE

The Maya migrants in Houston come from farming and artisanal communities situated in Guatemala's western highlands. As Table 1 shows, over 71 percent of the migrants in the

TABLE I

Community of Origin by Gender

	MEN		WOMEN		TOTAL	
	%	NO.	%	NO.	%	NO.
Guatemala City	2.4	1	—	—	1.3	1
DEPARTMENT OF TOTONICAPÁN						
Municipio of Ojo de Agua	4.8	2	3.1	1	4.0	3
Municipio of San Antonio de Belén	4.8	2	12.5	4	8.1	6
Municipio of San Pedro	73.8	31	68.7	22	71.6	53
DEPARTMENT OF QUEZALTENANGO						
Municipio of San Rafael	11.9	5	12.5	4	12.2	9
DEPARTMENT OF EL QUICHÉ						
Municipio of San Juan de Dios	2.4	1	3.1	1	2.7	2
TOTAL	100.1	42	99.9	32	99.9	74

study's sample come from a series of villages in the municipio, or township, of San Pedro, located in the Department of Totonicapán. The majority of the remaining migrants come from close-by municipios, also located in the highland Department of Totonicapán, and from the neighboring Department of Quezaltenango.

The municipio has long been recognized as the culturally relevant unit of analysis for studying Maya communities in the highlands (Tax 1937; Watanabe 1984; Nash 1967). Like most Maya communities in the western highlands, the municipio of San Pedro is a distinct social unit. Its geographic parameters are clearly marked; the town center serves as the administrative, social, and religious headquarters; its crafts are localized; its people speak a local variety of the Quiché language; and women wear a distinctive dress. Its inhabitants share an ethnic identity that sets them apart from other highland communities. As described below, San Pedro participates in a highland rotating market system based on the municipio's artisanal and farming specialization. Thus, the cultural cohesiveness of the community is reflected in its distinctive dialect, crafts, and dress, which differ from those of neighboring municipios.

The municipio of San Pedro covers an area of 40.2 square miles and is situated along the banks of a river in the southernmost section of the Department of Totonicapán. Nestled high in the Sierra Madre mountains, the climate is predominantly cool and dry, except for the daily afternoon shower during the rainy season. The picturesque meadows and valleys are dotted with tile-roofed adobe houses and milpas (cornfields). Corn is the predominant crop in the area. The municipio comprises the town center of San Pedro, seven cantones (hamlets), and three smaller farming settlements, located within a healthy walking distance of the town center. The 1981 census, the most recent and reliable census for the area, lists the municipio as having approximately 19,970 inhabitants, 93 percent of them of Maya origin. Most of the San Pedro Maya (83 percent) live in the municipio's cantones (DGE, 1984).

The interactions of everyday life flow between the town center and the surrounding cantones. Most of the town residents own milpas in the cantones and make the daily trip to work their land. The town of San Pedro is the administrative and political headquarters of the municipio. Facing the town plaza is an historic Catholic church, which was erected at the turn of the 18th century, shortly after the municipio was established. The mayor's office, the municipio's police headquarters, and several modest Protestant temples are all within short walking distance of the town plaza.

In addition to being the religious and judicial center of the municipio, San Pedro provides many services that attract the rural population. The weekly Sunday market and annual fiesta are held in the town plaza. San Pedro also provides a post office, a recently established international courier service, a health clinic, and transportation lines in and out of the municipio. The town is also the commercial center and includes several bakeries, manufacturers of pine caskets, eating establishments, general stores, a movie theater, herb shops, tailor shops, gasoline stations, bike stores, and cobbler shops.

San Pedro's economy is similar to other rural economies in Totonicapán which continue to experience change. By the late 19th century, most Maya households in the municipios of Totonicapán had shifted their primary economic activities from agricultural production for self-sufficiency to specialized commodity production (Smith 1984). Being the most densely settled department in Guatemala (Veblen 1982), Totonicapán's land tenure pattern reflects dramatic *minifundia* (SMO) (extreme subdivision of land into small plots). The major crop is corn, followed by wheat and a variety of local vegetables. Corn relies on the agricultural system of milpa, a shifting cultivation process in which corn is strategically and carefully grown alongside other crops such as tomatoes and onions.

By 1950 the municipios of Totonicapán had established their own rotating marketing system, one operated entirely by Maya traders who move mainly Maya produced commodities throughout the region (Smith 1984). Designed on a rotating basis, each of the participating municipios takes a turn at hosting the marketplace. The Totonicapán Maya travel to the various municipios to buy, sell, and trade their products. From 1950 to 1975 the number of marketplaces in the region increased from 150 to more than 300 (Smith 1984:61). By the mid-seventies, residents in many of the municipios in Totonicapán had become increasingly dependent on the market for their consumption and producer goods, and subsistence agriculture evolved into a supplementary activity for most households (Smith 1984:67). Census

NESTOR RODRÍGUEZ

Hernan, a Houston migrant, with his parents in front of their home and milpa in San Pedro.

data on sources of income for the entire Department of Totonicapán (the smallest unit for which data are available) show that in 1983, approximately 34 percent of the population were working primarily in agriculture while 60 percent were involved primarily in trade and artisanal production (Smith 1984:68).

In San Pedro, most households own and farm their own milpas, supplying much of the corn-based food consumed by their members. In addition, many households raise sheep for the production of woven fabric, and some of the population in the rural settlements raise dairy cattle for the market and pigs for local butcher shops. Despite agricultural involvement, very few households in the municipio depend solely on their land for income; most households have members engaged in different forms of production. Subsistence farming is supplemented by small specialized enterprises (e.g., bakeries, tailor shops) that primarily utilize family labor and by household production of localized crafts (e.g., woven garments, pottery, pine furniture, embroidered blouses). Crafts are sold or traded directly by the producers or by local traders at the daily highland markets that link the various highland communities economically.

Weaving and tailoring are the dominant artisanal occupations in San Pedro. The male members of the households control the production process. Approximately 20 percent of all skirt cloth produced in Guatemala is woven by San Pedro weavers, most of whom are men (Smith 1984). The female role in the production of garments worn in San Pedro is generally restricted to embroidering the trim of *huipiles,* the loose-fitting blouse worn by the women. The artisanal base of the highland economies, however, is declining. As rapid inflation has stifled the purchasing power of the peasants over the past few decades, the demand for woven goods has slackened. As younger women in the region rely increasingly on less expensive, ready-to-wear Western clothing and machine-woven cloth, the demand for hand-woven fabric has diminished substantially. The downturn in the weaving industry has been counterbalanced by a booming tailoring industry, which produces the bulk of the clothing worn by peasant men in the region. It is estimated that as much as 50 percent of the ready-made clothing is produced in the Department of Totonicapán (Smith 1984).

Over the past decade, political conflict in the region has also had a serious impact on the agricultural and artisanal bases of the Maya economy. The western highlands were the site of much government counterinsurgency and guerrilla activity in the 1980s (Hagan 1986; Americas Watch 1984; Dalli Sante 1983; Black, Jamail, and Chinchilla 1984; Loucky 1992), and many of the area's artisans and farmers were forced to flee their homes, migrating as refugees to Mexico and the United States (Hagan 1986; Manz 1988; Ferris 1987). The most notable Maya refugee groups are the Quiché from El

Quiché and the Kanjobal from Huehuetenango, who began fleeing their homes in the northwestern highlands of Guatemala in response to government repression in the 1980s. They have since taken shelter in United Nations refugee camps in southern Mexico or ventured farther north to the United States, where they have formed communities in Houston, Los Angeles, and Florida (Loucky 1988, 1992; Burns 1989, 1993; and Rodríguez 1987).

Fortunately, San Pedro Totonicapán escaped the worst guerrilla or counterinsurgency activity during this period. Political activities in the region did, however, limit the capacity of many of San Pedro's artisans to trade and sell their products in the regional markets. While the San Pedro Maya in Houston overwhelmingly identify themselves as economic migrants, artisans in the community speak of how they were forced to limit trade in some area markets for fear of being harassed or forcibly recruited by counterinsurgency and guerrilla forces. Thus, the nearby presence of guerrilla and counterinsurgency activities constrained their ability to participate in the regional market system. This, along with increasing inflation, which diminished the purchasing power of the quetzal (the Guatemalan currency) in the 1980s, forced many households in San Pedro to seek other sources of income, one of which is wage labor in Houston.

Recent decades have also witnessed a pattern of diminishing Maya cultural practices in all of the western highlands, including the decreasing use of Maya dialects and the replacement of traditional dress with Western clothing by most of the Maya men and a rapidly growing number of women. These changes notwithstanding, San Pedro migrants come from an area that continues to maintain a relatively rich level of Maya culture. This is not surprising, given that as recently as 1982, 95 percent of the inhabitants of the Department of Totonicapán were primarily Quiché-speaking Maya (Veblen 1982). Thus, cultural continuity is evident in the continued use of the

Quiché language and in an economy that includes artisans, traders, and small farmers (Smith 1988; Rodríguez 1989a).

The Maya communities that exist in the western highlands continue to change. They are no longer the insular formations described by early anthropologists (Redfield 1934; Tax 1937). Recent studies, however, continue to reveal a resilient community intrinsic to the highlands. Despite the sweeping economic and cultural changes that Maya communities have experienced under four and a half centuries of Spanish and Ladino (non-Maya Guatemalan) rule, they continue to retain an ethnic localism that, while no longer insular or closed, makes them distinctive (Warren 1978; Brintnall 1979; Burgos-Debray 1984; Watanabe 1984, 1990).

The municipio is still used as the culturally relevant unit of analysis for studying continuity and change among Maya communities in the highlands of western Guatemala (e.g., Wagley 1941; Reina 1957; Nash 1967; Watanabe 1984; Smith 1988). We are only just beginning to recognize the expression of Maya identity and culture on Maya immigrant formation outside the highlands (Burns 1989; Loucky 1988, 1992; Rodríguez 1987; Rodríguez and Hagan 1989). In the remaining pages of this chapter, we shall see the San Pedro Maya's expression of their self-identity in a new home, exemplified by those cultural features of San Pedro which have been reproduced in the Houston setting.

ᛗ REPRODUCING AND TRANSFORMING MAYA CULTURE IN HOUSTON
Belonging to a Common Community of Origin

Given the intrinsic nature of community in the highlands of Guatemala, it is not surprising that the most important social tie that bonds the Maya migrants in Houston is a common community of origin (i.e., the municipio of San Pedro Totonicapán). In an unknown and often threatening new environment, the presence of more than a thousand kin and friends from the same home town or from neighboring cantones eases the cultural adjustment and promotes a sense of belonging among these immigrants. In fact, by organizing their migration at the cantón level, households in Houston become an extension of the community of origin. Marisela, one of the more established members of the community in Houston, conveys the cohesive nature of the community of origin and its importance in promoting ethnic identity and enhancing group solidarity among the San Pedro Maya in Houston:

> There are few strangers in the community. Some I know better than others because they are closer relatives or we lived near each other or worked together in the milpas. As you know, not all of us come from the same village but we know each other in many other ways; from church, from school, our parents or brothers and sisters know one another. Many of us are related to one another. We are all from Totonicapán. We are all indígenas [the term the Houston Maya use to refer to themselves when in the company of non-Maya persons, myself included]. There are *naturales* and there are *hamus* [Spanish and phonetic Quiché terms for indigenous and non-indigenous, respectively]. I can remember when all the indígenas in Houston were from San Pedro only. Now there are indígenas from all over Totonicapán in Houston. I didn't know them all in Guate[mala] but I meet them at church or at someone's home and we find out that maybe our grandparents are related. So, even though we may not have lived in the same village in Guate, we recognize each other and we know each other. I am sure you can recognize one of us too [she laughs]. We are Maya outside and inside. Our lives and our children's lives will be different in Houston. We may change, but we will always be indígena. I know that some of the indígena try to hide

their identity here, as if they don't want Americans to know who they are. Some do that in Guate as well, but most of us are very proud of our identity and our culture. We are trying to keep it alive. It doesn't matter if I cut my hair or wear short American dresses, I will always be indígena.

As Marisela notes, initially the Totonicapán Maya in Houston constituted a single network. Over the years, however, as returning migrants spread the news of their success in Houston to nearby cantones, the social networks tying the highlands and the Houston community have increased and diversified. Once consisting primarily of single males from San Pedro, today networks linking the highlands to Houston may be as diverse as a group of ten people from one extended family to a group of female friends from several villages. Despite the development of more numerous and more complex household, friendship, and cantón networks, at some level all networks interact because their members share a common Maya origin.

Typically, members of the various networks come together for life-cycle events of members in the larger community, such as the arrival of new migrants, quinceañeras, funerals, birthdays, and weddings. In the case of an unexpected crisis, the whole community comes together to provide support. During my early months in the field, for example, one of the Maya in Houston became ill and died rather suddenly. Overnight, his wife and young child, who had just recently joined him in Houston, were left penniless. The community response was dramatic. Several of his coworkers and friends went from household to household in the community, collecting donations to pay the cost of transporting the body back home to Guatemala and providing some temporary financial assistance to his family. Several days after the young man's death, while I was paying my respects to the widow, I witnessed a steady stream of Maya who dropped by to offer their condolences and assistance; then a group of men arrived with the community donation. Clearly, the hardship placed on families in Houston and Guatemala is eased by such efforts on the part of the Houston Maya community.

Women and the Reproduction of Material Symbols

The reproduction of cultural symbols of Maya identity can also serve to enhance group solidarity and community formation and, ultimately, to ease adaptation. Perhaps most notable among the various cultural symbols that have found their way to Houston are the Maya garments characteristic of the women of Guatemala's western highlands. The Maya women from this region adorn themselves in the customary *huipil* and *corte*. The huipil is a loose-fitting blouse trimmed in bright, colorful embroidery work; the corte is an ankle-length woven skirt, usually in red or blue, which is trimmed along the hemline with elaborate embroidery work and velvet.

The San Pedro Maya women in Houston, especially the older women, have retained these traditional garments, albeit with some modifications. For example, much of the embroidery and skirt cloth is now manufactured, rather than hand-stitched and woven on looms as in the past (Smith 1988). Moreover, the diminishing purchasing power of the quetzal has made it difficult for younger Maya women to afford the more expensive traditional dress.

In Houston, though, use of traditional Maya dress is reproduced. Although traditional dress is rarely worn by women at work during the week (except by newcomers who have not yet purchased Western clothing), most adorn themselves in the huipil and corte when they are among members of their community, when they are at home in their own neighborhood (which is usually on the weekends), and always when participating in such cultural and community events as fiestas, Sunday dinners, church meetings, or life-cycle celebrations like birthdays and weddings.

Wearing huipil and corte, mother and daughter pose in their Houston neighborhood.

The Totonicapán Maya women in Houston display an enormous sense of ethnic and locale identification through the regular use of the huipil and corte. They are enthusiastic about relating the historical and geographic context of the different designs that frame their garments. Each municipio in Totonicapán, as elsewhere in the highlands, has its own local design. Maya communities in the highlands are distinguished from one another on the basis of the huipil and corte. In fact, the huipil and corte remain among the most important symbols of native identity in the highlands of Guatemala (Smith 1988:230).

In Houston, too, the Maya home communities are distinguishable by the use of different huipils and cortes. For example, the cortes worn by women migrants from

Quezaltenango are full and pleated, with a drawstring, and hang just below the knee. These contrast with the ankle-length cortes worn by the women of San Pedro, which are straight and narrow and wrapped in layers around the lower body before being closed at the waist with a colorful belt. The cultural importance of the huipil and corte is made clear by Carmen, here describing preparations for her family's first visit to San Pedro since receiving their temporary residence cards:

> Everything is almost ready for the trip. María [her oldest daughter] will be staying with my sister-in-law here [María's residency papers were not ready in time for her to make the trip]. Ana [her U.S.–born child] will be going back with us. We are all very excited, but I am also worried because I have not yet received Ana's huipil and corte. She must arrive in San Pedro wearing them.

As Carmen's remarks show, the huipil and corte not only promote communal identity among Maya migrants in Houston but, equally important, they facilitate the reintegration of returning migrants into the home community. This is particularly important for the younger girls in the community, especially for U.S.–born daughters such as Ana who have never made the trip home. For this group, the huipil and corte ease their introduction to the home culture.

Also evidenced by Carmen's comments is the fact that one of the most significant aspects of material culture found back home (i.e., artisanal production) is not being reproduced in Houston. Totonicapán has long been recognized as the seat of artisanal production in Guatemala. Generations of Totonicapán men have woven by hand, or more recently by machine, the garments worn by Maya women throughout the highlands and have manufactured the bulk of the westernized clothing worn by most of the men (McBryde 1945; Smith 1984, 1988). Similarly, generations of Totonicapán women have embroidered the trim of these garments.

NESTOR RODRÍGUEZ

*In San Pedro for the first time, Ana, the U.S.-born Maya
daughter of Carmen and Juan, shucks corn for the preparation
of tamales.*

Unfortunately, the occupational structure in Houston does
not allow for the maintenance of artisanal production. None
of the Totonicapán Maya in Houston has been able to transfer their artisanal and farming skills to the city's oil- and
service-based economy. Their concentration in Houston's
service industries contrasts with patterns of work found in
other Maya communities in the United States. For example,
the Kanjobal Maya in Los Angeles, many of whom were
tailors and weavers in their home communities in the northwestern region of the Department of Huehuetenango, have
made inroads into the city's garment industry (Loucky 1988).
Similarly, in Indiantown, Florida, the Kanjobal Maya bring
their farming skills to the sugarcane fields; a textile cooperative, which draws on the crafts produced by the migrants, has
also been established there (Burns 1989).

Because the Maya men in Houston have not been able to

transfer their artisanal skills as weavers or tailors into the Houston labor market, the women must rely on long distance production; that is, they must have the garment produced at home and sent to Houston via courier (discussed below) from the San Pedro community. Although most of the migrant women in the community own several sets of these garments, passed down from their mothers and grandmothers, it is common practice to purchase a new one yearly. The children, on the other hand, depend exclusively on theirs being sent from San Pedro. Yet, despite the difficulty of obtaining traditional garments for growing children in the United States, I do not know one woman or female child in the Houston community who does not own her own huipil and corte.

The role of women in the community as primary reproducers of Maya culture is also seen in the use of other cultural symbols. For the most part, as in the highlands, migrant women rarely cut their hair, wearing it greased in two long *trenzas* (braids) tied together with brightly colored cloth woven through the trenzas. The notable exceptions to this practice are school-age girls in the community, who insist on looking "more like other children in school" and who complain about being "kidded" for their greased hair. On occasion, a more established migrant in the community will also westernize her hairstyle, but not without community consequences. Monica, a thirty-one-year-old Maya migrant from the municipio of San Antonio de Belén who has been living in Houston since 1981, told me what happened after she had her hair cut to shoulder length and trimmed with bangs:

> Some of the women in the community here in Houston didn't like it that I cut my hair, but were too respectful to say anything to me. Maybe because I am one of a few not from San Pedro. But when I went home for a visit, [the first of several since she went through the legalization process] my mother, sisters, and friends were very angry

and sad about what I had done. I think they felt it was disrespectful to my culture. But I won't change it. This is also my home and culture, and I want to feel free to do what other women do here.

Monica is one of a handful of older, never-married women in the community. Interestingly, she is one of the few women in the community who express a desire to remain here permanently and marry a non-Maya. She believes her age acts as a barrier to her returning home and marrying a Maya, and she feels it is more important to adapt and adjust to her new culture than to perpetuate the traditions of her old culture.

In the Totonicapán Maya homes, other material symbols are reproduced to bond the household with visiting community members. These include the elaborate preparation of traditional foods from their region and municipio (e.g., *estufado*, *caldos*, and potato and rice *tamales*). Because most of the women work as live-in domestics during the week (to be discussed in Chapter Three), preparation of these regional foods is restricted to weekend meals in their households and to special church and other community events. Although serving traditional food is limited to these events, the preparation usually unites groups of women, and the meals draw many of the Maya together on a regular basis.

Religion

Some cultural symbols are both reproduced and transformed. Religious behavior is one of these, and in the Houston Maya community that behavior reflects the changing nature of religious identity in the municipio of San Pedro. The recent evangelization of much of the western highland region of Guatemala, once a predominantly Catholic region, has created potential religious distinctions within formerly homogeneous communities. The first substantial stream of Protestant missionaries arrived in the region after World War II, and their presence escalated following the 1976 earthquake. Unlike the Catholic clergy, who were targets of rural violence, the Protestant clergy were largely left alone because they were mostly conservative, evangelical fundamentalists who engaged in little activity that threatened the established social order. Their ability to offer food, medical care, or housing is a significant inducement to the rural Maya.

In 1982, following his conversion from Catholicism to evangelical Protestantism, President Efraín Ríos Montt invited religious workers and clergy who had been driven out of the country by violence to return. By 1982, over 20 percent of the Guatemalan population claimed to be affiliated with some Protestant sect (Kluck 1983). Interestingly, the surge in Protestantism in the highlands was not among mainstream Protestant denominations, but among small fundamentalist sects. Today, it is not unusual to find small Maya communities divided into Catholic, mainline Protestant, and fundamentalist congregations. By the 1980s, 6,800 Protestant congregations, divided into more than a hundred denominations, had sprung up throughout the country (Kluck 1983).

Evangelicals are not oriented toward formal, doctrinal orthodoxy; instead, they emphasize the individual believer's personal relationship with God. Unlike the mainstream Catholics and Protestants, they are not concerned with large-scale social reform and political change. Rather, they are much more individualistic and family-oriented in focus. This has been especially appealing to the Mayas in San Pedro, who distance themselves from political identification and shy away from political discourse. In a country where Catholic clergy are often believed to be sympathetic to guerrilla activities, many of the Maya find it safer to be affiliated with a Protestant sect. Nonetheless, the surge in Protestant sects implies a break with more traditional members of the Maya communities in Guatemala and therefore may develop into a source of division among the Maya in Houston as the period of settlement grows. For example, among the Konjobal Maya in

Florida, Seventh Day Adventists have resettled to the West Palm Beach area, while the Catholic Konjobal have remained in Indiantown (Burns 1993).

Before the 1970s, the town center of San Pedro housed two Catholic churches. While no data are available on religious affiliation in the San Pedro population, a look at the different religious organizations sheds some light on conversion in the municipio. As of 1990, one of the Catholic churches had been closed because of a diminishing congregation, while more than nine Protestant churches had been established during the previous decade. Moreover, the Protestant population is a diverse group, including Seventh Day Adventists, Church of God followers, and members of lesser-known evangelical sects. By 1993, a handful of Protestant missionaries from the United States were living in Maya households and were actively engaged in promoting education and other services in the town center of San Pedro.

Most of the Protestant missions and churches in San Pedro have close ties with U.S.–based institutions. Consequently, Maya migrants found it relatively easy to reproduce their religious preferences in the United States. In Houston, the migrants attend two different Protestant churches (Seventh Day Adventist, Church of God) and one Roman Catholic church. One of the Protestant churches is actually a community-formed church and will be elaborated on in Chapter Three.

Table 2, which lists religious affiliation and participation of the 74 in the study sample, shows the heterogeneity of religious identity among the Maya in Houston. While all these Maya identify with some religion, the majority are Protestant, which reflects the dramatic increase in fundamentalist religions in Guatemala since 1960, especially during the 1960s and 1970s (Brintnall 1979). Heterogeneity of religious behavior has also been found among the Kanjobal Maya in Florida; in a survey conducted in 1986 in Indiantown,

TABLE 2
Religious Identification by Gender

	MEN		WOMEN		TOTAL	
	%	NO.	%	NO.	%	NO.
RELIGIOUS AFFILIATION						
Catholic	47.6	20	28.1	9	39.2	29
Protestant	52.4	22	71.9	23	60.8	45
TOTAL	100.0	42	100.0	32	100.0	74
CHURCH PARTICIPATION						
Catholic	35.7	15	18.7	6	28.4	21
Protestant	45.2	19	68.7	22	55.4	41
None	19.0	8	12.5	4	16.2	12
TOTAL	99.9	42	99.9	32	100.0	74

it was found that 37 percent of the eighty-nine families surveyed reported being followers of the Seventh Day Adventists and other Protestant groups, another 36 percent reported being Catholic, and the remaining 27 percent said they followed no religion (Miralles 1986).

Table 2 also shows that the proportion of women who are Protestant is greater than that of men. Church participation (service attendance and regular participation in church activities) also varies by gender, with women being the most active group. The Maya in Houston report that church-related activities were central to community and family life back home. This was especially true for Protestant migrants, who told me that, in addition to weekly services, *hermanos* (brothers and sisters of the same mission) met at one another's homes on a frequent basis to discuss Bible verses, a practice that continues among Houston Maya households. Men and women provide different explanations for why men participate less in church activities in Houston than women.

The demands of their jobs and lack of transportation are the most common reasons given by Catholic as well as Protestant men in the community. Women, on the other hand, who share similar job and transportation restrictions, argue that men do not attend services or participate at the level they did back home because they are no longer under the watchful eye of their parents and other older kin. Many of the women agreed with Lidia, one of the most active women in the community Protestant mission, when she offered her thoughts on the matter:

> Those men who have recently arrived in Houston attend services more. In fact, some even convert to our church; but things change with time. They start drinking [sobriety is required of the congregation]. I think they change because they're on their own, away from the elders in the community. Without their parents, they may break the rules of the church. It's different with the *hermanas* [sisters of the same church]. We have the community and, most important, our children to think about. The church is where they learn Quiché and about our culture. We enjoy our time at church. It's a time when the women come together. Unlike us, the men work together, and they have their soccer. We have our meetings at church.

Lidia's comments suggest that men are more likely than women to stray from the normative structure guiding religious behavior, once they leave the home community. In most cases, the men in the community settle in the Houston area before sending for their spouses and children. Being alone and exposed to life-styles foreign to community life back home certainly provides for alternative behaviors (in this case, drinking and not attending church services). Women, on the other hand, rely more on the community church in the settlement process. Moreover, apart from the services themselves, activities in the community church solely involve and are organized by the women. For example, community meals for special occasions (e.g., fund-raising, quinceañeras, weddings, birthdays) are prepared by the women in the church kitchen, and a special Bible-reading session is held weekly for mothers and their daughters. Again, the theme of women as reproducers of traditional culture emerges.

Language

I learned Quiché at home. All indígenas do. But beginning with my generation, we learned Spanish at school. In Guate, Quiché is always spoken at home with the older members of the household and Spanish is spoken outside the home. This is especially true for those of us living in the *pueblo* [town], as we were most likely to go to school. This doesn't mean our Spanish is so good. Most of us can't read or write it [Spanish], as we never went more than three or four years to school. What's sad is that many of the young indígenas do not try to use Quiché anymore. The problem is that it's no longer necessary except with the elderly in the community who speak no Spanish. Sure, there are certain words we only express in Quiché, but it's more important to speak Spanish now. This can sometimes be a problem. Last month when I took my family home, it was very sad to see that Luz [the daughter of the Maya man speaking] could barely communicate with my mother-in-law. Luz understands some Quiché, but can barely speak it. My mother-in-law understands Spanish, but can't speak it. What can we do? We've taught her some Quiché, but we're also trying to teach her Spanish at home and then she must speak English at school. It's a lot for a child, I think, and like so many other aspects of Guatemala, she is beginning to reject Quiché.

Macro is one of the older and more established members

of the community. As his comments convey, it is much more difficult for the Maya to reproduce certain cultural symbols in their new home. The Quiché language, one of the most important cultural symbols of ethnicity in the Department of Totonicapán, is not being reproduced in Houston. Although the majority of the Maya migrants in Houston know and use Quiché, it is the Spanish language that characteristically structures interaction within the community, especially among the more established members.

Some of the Maya were quick to point out that although Spanish is more commonly spoken throughout the community, Quiché is spoken on occasion, but usually only among themselves. They refrain from using the Quiché language in the presence of non-Maya, not wanting to draw attention to their Maya origin. Several key informants, however, maintained that Quiché continues to shape interaction among close friends and adult kin in the household, workplace, and almost always among women during church-related activities. It is usually the language that guides conversation about life back home. The men report that among the Maya work crews, Quiché is spoken informally, often in the context of jesting among themselves or discussing something they do not want a non-Maya to overhear.

It is clear that the use of Quiché is not widespread among the Maya in Houston and that the potential for maintaining even minimal use of the language among second-generation migrants is slight. Several factors may contribute to this transformation from Quiché to Spanish, including 1. the diminishing use of Quiché in the municipio of San Pedro; 2. the age structure of the Houston Maya community; 3. the increasing presence of U.S.–born children in the community who speak English and Spanish; 4. the predominantly Spanish-speaking labor force within which the Houston Maya work; and 5. the preference among the Houston Maya not to draw attention to their Maya origin.

The use of Quiché has been declining in all municipios in

the Department of Totonicapán in recent years. Visits to the home community of San Pedro by myself and my research partner, Nestor Rodríguez, found its use diminishing. In the municipio of San Pedro, Quiché is spoken primarily by those living in the rural settlements around town and by the aged of the community. Increasingly, Spanish is spoken by the younger Maya and by the town inhabitants.

Factors associated with the migration experience also limit the reproduction of the Quiché language in Houston. The young age structure of the Maya community limits the potential for maintenance and reproduction. For example, seventy-eight percent of the adults in the community sample are under thirty years of age, and only 3 percent are above the age of forty. The absence of older cohorts in the community lessens the need to maintain the Quiché language in Houston, while the presence of a predominantly young and economically active population among the Maya in Houston requires greater use of Spanish. In an urban and Hispanic setting like Houston, interaction crosses ethnic boundaries in the workplace, at church, on the soccer field, and in residential settings.

The increasing presence of U.S.–born children and school-age children in the community also challenges the perpetuation of Quiché in the community. In the beginning years of community settlement, Quiché instruction was formalized into a weekly event at church gatherings of women and children. However, with the increasing number of children attending school and learning English, church efforts have waned and parental efforts are concentrated on maintaining the use of Spanish, rather than Quiché, at home. This is not to say that efforts to teach Quiché to the children have been abandoned. The children in the community are still exposed to it at church and some parents, especially those from the cantones, do stress Quiché in the home. Still, an overall pattern of decreasing use at the community level is clear.

Loucky (1988) likewise acknowledges the diminishing use

of Kanjobal among the Kanjobal Maya in Los Angeles. In urban centers characterized by large, heterogeneous Latino populations, like Los Angeles and Houston, knowledge of Spanish and English becomes essential. In contrast, in a more rural and isolated setting, such as Indiantown, Florida, the Kanjobal language continues to flourish (Burns 1988). While the Maya in all three communities are being pushed to speak Spanish and English, maintenance of the native language reflects the transformation in language in the home communities as well as features unique to the migration and settlement experience. In contrast to the majority of the Kanjobal Maya, who spoke only Kanjobal upon arrival in the United States, most of the Totonicapán Maya arrived with a knowledge of both Quiché and Spanish.

To explain the differences between Kanjobal language-use patterns in Indiantown, Los Angeles, and Houston, one must look beyond transformation in language patterns in the home community to the migration experience itself. The Kanjobal Maya in Indiantown migrated in large family and community groups and settled in a small farming community. The presence of wider support from the older segment of the community facilitates cultural maintenance among the youth, who are most likely to reject use of their native language. In contrast, the multiethnic labor markets of Houston and Los Angeles require a knowledge of both Spanish and English.

♦♦ A MAYA STRATEGY FOR CULTURAL EXCHANGE

Reproducing cultural symbols associated with the home community enhances solidarity among the Totonicapán Maya in Houston. Symbols of Maya identity also serve to remind migrants of their community of origin and promote a sense of belonging to a community in Houston. Some cultural features of the home community (food preference, religious behavior) are easily reproduced in Houston; others are transformed (language use and dress). Still others are lost entirely (artisanal production).

The difficulty associated with reproducing some cultural dimensions of the home community in Houston was eased by the early development of a courier service. Prior to the acquisition of legal residence through IRCA, only a handful in the community dared to make the risky trip back home for a visit. For the undocumented Maya, the journey consisted of crossing two borders with no papers and passing through highland areas of political activity. The few brave men who made the undocumented journey did so either to escort a spouse into the United States or to bring back a U.S.–born child to be raised in Guatemala.

In the absence of frequent travel back and forth, the Totonicapán community developed an organizational strategy to maintain cultural exchange between the two communities. Six couriers, men and women alike, make monthly trips between the two communities. All six have visas, which allowed them to travel with little difficulty. In the following description of a typical monthly trip, Jaime, a young man from San Pedro and one of the more established couriers in the community, highlights the courier's role in facilitating cultural exchange:

> I try to locate another courier or person in the community to drive with me. This lets me bring down a truck, which I sell in Guatemala, and also allows me to bring more things to San Pedro. Usually, I just let the community know when I am leaving, and they come to me with things to be sent home. Things such as dollars, cassette recordings [made by household members in Houston for immediate family and other kin back home], televisions, and blenders. I charge ten dollars for a cassette and fifty

dollars for a television. Once all the items are delivered to people back home, I start loading things up in Guatemala and bring them back to Houston. I usually bring back cassettes from homes in San Pedro, huipiles and cortes, spices, wedding bands for weddings here. Sometimes I bring people back with me, but I prefer not to. It's not worth the risk. The "coyotes" can do that.

Clearly the couriers make a handsome little profit from these monthly trips. While their motives are principally monetary, it is nonetheless clear that this service performs several important functions in the process of cultural exchange and mutual community development. For one thing, it serves to reproduce some dimensions of Maya culture in Houston and to maintain ethnic culture in San Pedro. Through the courier service, the Maya in Houston receive regular supplies of ethnic clothing, spices and other foods from Guatemala, and traditional gold jewelry worn by the women and used in life-cycle events (e.g., traditional wedding rings and earrings). Similarly, money sent by migrants in Houston helps to produce and purchase traditional clothing worn by Maya women and assists in financing the "fiesta titular" (annual fiesta), held each July in San Pedro.

Remittances sent to Guatemala also support local economic and social development among households in the home community. Couriers bring aspects of U.S. material culture (e.g., high-tech appliances) into the home community, as well as pooled funds to furnish outfits for the San Pedro soccer team and to maintain the local health clinic in San Pedro. Remittances from Houston also pay for children's education in San Pedro. Over 20 percent of the individuals in my sample mentioned funding their children's private schooling in Guatemala through wages earned in Houston. The social value placed on this practice, not to mention the extensive role of couriers in sustaining relations between the

NESTOR RODRÍGUEZ

Appliances and other items sent from Houston fill a home in San Pedro.

two communities, was displayed at a recent fiesta. The hostess, a recently separated Maya women in her mid-forties, invited community members to a fiesta in her home to celebrate the high school graduation of her son in San Pedro. The guests, numbering close to fifty persons, arrived with a variety of gifts for her son (e.g., a watch, shirts, a calculator). The fiesta took on the form of a ceremony as the hostess opened the events with a speech in which she thanked the Houston community for furthering the education of the children in Totonicapán. She went on to say how proud she was to be the first San Pedro Maya mother to have made an event like this possible. At the close of the fiesta, the courier arrived to pick up the gifts, which would be loaded into his truck and taken to the son of the hostess on the following day.

Members of the home community will make the trip north for special occasions, serving as *padrinos* (Godparents) for the bride or helping to celebrate the quinceañera. It is customary not only that the padrino be from the same locale, but that he be of a higher social class than the bride or groom. In a 1987 wedding, the owners of a Totonicapán garment factory, which employs a substantial number of the San Pedro community in Guatemala, made the trip to Houston for the sole purpose of giving away the bride. This custom provides future financial security for the bride's family in San Pedro and ensures the bride employment should she ever return home.

Prior to IRCA, few of the migrants returned home on a regular basis, both because of their undocumented status and because of the physical distance between the two communities. Despite these constraints, social interaction between households in Guatemala and Houston was extensive and played an important role in the reproduction of indígena culture and in community development in both communities. Whether the legalization of some members of the Houston community increases or decreases opportunities for cultural exchange is a question to be addressed in Chapter Five. One might hypothesize that legal status increases cultural exchanges and maintains ethnic identity, as community members can return home legally on a more frequent basis.

On the other hand, observations of the behavior of the Maya settled in Houston suggest several barriers to the long-term reproduction of Maya culture there. Because the Totonicapán women in Houston are the primary reproducers of Maya culture, future cultural reproduction will depend largely on the cultural behavior of their daughters. Identity among the children in the Houston community, however, is shifting as they become increasingly incorporated into the Latino populations at school. Evidence of such shifting identity is expressed both in their unwillingness to wear traditional Maya garments in Houston and in their resistance to sustaining the Quiché language. Maya identity is also shifting within the community as newcomers make their way into the

Houston labor market, where they work in unskilled jobs alongside Mexicans and non-Guatemalan Central Americans. In their homeland, the Maya are the only indigenous group. As Burns (1993) observed in his study of the Kanjobal Maya in Indiantown, Florida, the Maya in the United States are becoming increasingly aware of their status as one of a great number of minority groups. Increasingly, then, we can expect their identity to become defined in relation to other minority groups such as Mexicans, Salvadorans, and Garifuna (from Belize and Honduras).

When Roberts wrote that "Ladino is the cultural and situational definition of a person who does not evidence by his speech, dress and location, membership in the Indian group" (Roberts 1974:231), he used cultural symbols to distinguish the two dominant ethnic groups of Guatemala. Just as these cultural distinctions are becoming less apparent in Guatemala, one must consider whether a long-term decline in the use of Maya cultural symbols among Totonicapán Maya in Houston may also blur distinctions of identity between Totonicapán Maya and other Central American migrant populations, especially non-Maya Guatemalans, in Houston.

CHAPTER THREE

THE SETTLEMENT PROCESS

EXCEPT FOR THE OCCASIONAL STREET SIGHTS OF WOMEN dressed in the picturesque designs and brilliant colors of the San Pedro and Quezaltenango huipiles and cortes, there are few visible signs (at least to the non-Maya eye) of a Maya population or community in Houston. This can be explained by the distinctive residential pattern that was adopted by the Totonicapán Maya during Houston's simultaneous economic downturn and development of a Central American neighborhood. Major and rapid changes in Houston's population structure and economy had a considerable influence on the residential pattern of immigrants, including the Totonicapán Maya (Hagan and Rodríguez, 1992).

⁜ DEMOGRAPHIC AND ECONOMIC CONTEXT

Beginning in the early 1980s, the composition of Houston's immigrant population began to change. Prior to this period, Houston's Latino population was overwhelmingly Mexican. Houston's economic base, first as a regional industrial center,

TABLE 3

Houston's Latino Population Growth, 1900–1990

YEAR	POPULATION SIZE
1900	1,000
1908	2,000
1920	6,000
1930	15,000
1940	20,000
1950	40,000
1960	75,000
1970	150,000
1980	280,000
1990	446,000

SOURCE: The 1900–1980 figures (from Shelton, Beth Ann, et al. 1989. *Houston: Growth and Decline in a Sunbelt Boomtown.* Philadelphia: Temple University Press [based on historical sources and on the 1970 and 1980 censuses]) are reprinted with permission. The 1990 figures are from U.S. Department of Commerce, Bureau of the Census. 1991. *1990 Census on Population and Housing.* The figures from 1900 to 1940 approximate the Mexican-origin population, which accounts for nearly all Latinos in the city. Figures from 1950 to 1980 represent Spanish-language, Spanish surname, or Hispanic-origin residents. Even at the time of the 1980 census, the Mexican-origin population represented an overwhelming majority (88 percent) of the city's Hispanics. The figures do not include the total undocumented Hispanic population.

NOTE: Only the incorporated city area is included. Data have been rounded to the nearest thousand.

beginning in the 1920s, then as the center of the world petrochemical industry in the 1960s and 1970s (Feagin 1988), has spurred a steady, century-long stream of working-class Mexican migrants to the area (see Table 3). Settling in areas nearby the industrial sectors of the east side (railways, ship channel, petroleum refineries, chemical plants, and other labor-intensive industries) where they worked, they created the well-known barrios of El Segundo, Magnolia, and Northside (Shelton et al. 1989). These barrios remained home to the majority of Houston's Latino population until the 1980s.

Beginning in the 1980s, large streams of new Latino populations began arriving in Houston. While undocumented Mexican workers continued to migrate to the area during this period, large numbers of Salvadorans, Guatemalans, and Hondurans (including families and single women) also made their way to Houston (Rodríguez 1987; Rodríguez and Hagan 1989). The recent large-scale immigration of Central Americans to Houston is evidenced in the dramatic, post-1980 growth of Houston's central-city Latino population, which increased from 281,331 in 1980 to 445,915 in 1990 (Shelton et al. 1989; Bureau of the Census 1990). The most recent census figures for the entire Houston metropolitan area place the number of Latinos at 707,536 (Sallee 1991).

The post-1980 migration of tens of thousands of Central Americans to the city coincided with a period of severe economic downturn in those petrochemical and construction industries which employed many of the Mexican workers during the days of economic prosperity. While past undocumented Mexicans have followed a heavy-industry employment pattern, field research indicates that Central American male workers are currently concentrated in the distributive and producer sectors of the service industry and that the majority of the Central American females work as domestics in the personal services sector (Rodríguez 1987; Rodríguez and Hagan 1989).

The settlement pattern of the Central American newcomers also contrasts with that of the more established Mexican immigrant population. While the majority of Mexican migrants to Houston settled in the city's traditional eastside barrios, many of the undocumented Central Americans have settled in the city's west side, where they would be close to the service industries in which they work and where they could find quality rental housing at an affordable price (Rodríguez and Hagan 1989). This distinctive residential choice has created new Hispanic zones in neighborhoods where, as recently as 1980, the census found no Latino presence.

Many of these westside neighborhoods, consisting of huge apartment complexes (a thousand units in some cases), were constructed during Houston's prosperous years of the 1960s and 1970s to house the growing number of Anglo and African-American office workers and professionals. By the mid-eighties Houston had over three thousand large apartment complexes, comprising 400,725 units (Smith 1989).

The boom years came to an abrupt halt in 1982, when the city entered a severe, five-year economic downturn. By 1987, Houston's economy had been hit by a 57 percent decrease in oil prices and a 77 percent reduction in active drilling rigs throughout the United States (Feagin 1988). The local repercussions of the downturn were disastrous. By 1987 unemployment had reached 10 percent, and the area had experienced a loss of over two hundred thousand jobs (Hagan and Rodríguez 1992; Rodríguez and Hagan 1992).

As others have discussed, economic crisis and accompanying restructuring begins in the primary circuit of capital (Beauregard 1989; Henderson and Castell 1987). Although the economic crisis originated in Houston's primary circuit of manufacturing capital and in oil- and petrochemical-related industries, it was not long before the area's secondary circuit of real-estate capital felt the shock (Hagan and Rodríguez 1992). The number of vacant residential units soared from 86,961 in 1981 to 220,709 in 1985. In 1986, 425 Houston-based real-estate firms were forced to file for bankruptcy. By 1987, vacancy rates in office buildings climbed to 28 percent, and residential-space vacancy rates had reached 18 percent (Smith 1989). Newly constructed large apartment complexes

One of the several apartment complexes that are home to the Maya in Houston.

were severely hit by the economic crisis; by the winter of 1987, economic vacancy rates (including physical vacancy and rental concessions) soared to 34.3 percent, an unprecedented high in the area's apartment industry (REVAC 1990). Some of the largest apartment complexes did not survive the crisis. From 1987 to 1989, almost 6,000 units were razed in Houston (Rosen 1990).

For others, salvation came in the form of undocumented migration. The post-1980 arrival of tens of thousands of Salvadorans, Guatemalans, and Hondurans enabled many of the area's apartment owners and managers to implement a strategy of tenant recomposition to survive the recession.

Westside apartment owners and managers were creative and bold in their efforts to draw the Central American newcomers to their vacated units. Recruitment strategies included bilingual advertising, changing apartment-complex names to names familiar in Spanish, free English classes, Spanish-speaking staff and maintenance personnel, and dramatic rent reductions (e.g., from six hundred dollars a month to two hundred dollars a month for a one-bedroom apartment). Central American newcomers, including the Totonicapán Maya, took advantage of the newly affordable housing and moved into relatively plush living arrangements. Designed for young professionals, many of the complexes featured such amenities as Jacuzzi, swimming pool, tennis courts, and laundry service.

The level of Latinization found in the new westside zones of Central American settlement is lower than that found in the traditional Mexican or eastside zones of the city, but appears to be increasing. New zones consist primarily of large clusters of Central American households scattered across blocks of apartment complexes interspersed with Anglos, African Americans, and Mexican Americans. There are visual signs indicating the development of a Central American neighborhood. These include groups of Latinos congregating on sidewalks and street corners, day-labor pools, Maya women in traditional garments, Central American grocery stores and music stores, Latino newsstands, a proliferation of Salvadoran restaurants, and a plethora of commercial signs and billboards written in Spanish.

Of the more than one hundred fifty thousand Central Americans who have settled in Houston's west side, Salvadorans constitute the largest group, numbering at least fifty thousand (Rodríguez and Hagan 1989) and possibly as many as a hundred thousand (Pensola 1986). Guatemalans constitute the second-largest Central American group in the city. Numbering less than half the size of the total Salvadoran population, Guatemalan immigrants consist both of Ladinos and indigenous Maya subgroups. The two highland Maya groups in the city are from El Quiché and Totonicapán. The Hondurans in Houston number fewer than fifteen thousand (Rodríguez and Hagan 1989) and comprise two populations, Ladino Hondurans and Garifuna (Black Caribs).

Interestingly, all three indigenous groups have strategical-ly settled in areas marginal to the greater Central American neighborhood. Basically, it is the presence of kin and friends from the home communities that has allowed the indigenous groups to do so. The Garifuna community is located at the greatest distance from the Central American neighborhood, having settled in one of Houston's African-American resi-dential districts. Despite the racial commonality, the Garifuna display a minimal level of interaction with their African-American neighbors. Much like the Totonicapán Maya, the Garifuna maintain cohesive network structures that help maintain their traditional culture, derived from the northern coast of Honduras (Rodríguez 1987). The Maya from the Department of El Quiché, a group whose settlement patterns we have only just begun to track, number over a thousand and reside in several westside apartment buildings located a few miles from the larger Central American neighborhood. Thus far, our research indicates that the El Quiché Maya keep social distance from other immigrant groups, including the Totonicapán Maya.

The presence of a critical mass—over a thousand kin and friends of similar ages and from the same home town—has also enabled the Totonicapán Maya to form settlement pock-ets on the outskirts of the Central American neighborhood. In this way they maintain a low profile, ethnic identity is enhanced, and they can take advantage of the nearby Latino services and low-cost housing in the area. As one of the members of the community explained, "Most of us prefer to keep to ourselves and not be together with the Salvadorans.

We are different. They drink and are loud. We really don't want to be identified with them."

This residential feature serves an important function in the establishment and reproduction of a community structure. Not only does it socially separate the Totonicapán Maya from other immigrant populations, thereby enhancing social interaction and promoting Maya identity among community members, but it also provides a host of social and economic resources (e.g., temporary housing, job information, transportation) for the newcomer Maya.

Most of the Totonicapán Maya live in clusters of households found in three large apartment complexes located on the fringe of the Central American neighborhood. (The exception to this pattern is found among the live-in domestics who reside in the community only over the weekend.) Approximately a hundred and twenty immigrant households, all within short walking distance of one another, serve as a rich source of social and economic resources for arriving migrants from San Pedro and its neighboring municipios in Totonicapán.

The close proximity of the households encourages daily interaction among the immigrants, leading to the development of networks within the residential confines of the Totonicapán community. These community networks provide financial and social resources for newcomers (e.g., transportation, temporary and permanent housing, news about potential jobs) and disseminate general community news (e.g., someone arriving or leaving, upcoming fiestas, life-cycle events) to all community members. News travels widely and rapidly through these neighborhood-based networks. The case of a 1988 immigration event illustrates the extensive reach of these networks within the neighborhood. Upon hearing of the U.S. State Department's 1988 decision to provide twenty thousand permanent resident visas through a lottery, I encouraged several of the Maya to apply and assisted them in filling out the required application. Within twenty-four hours of assisting the first immigrant with the application, over thirty others in the community were knocking on my door, requesting similar assistance.

᛭ TRANSFORMATIONS IN KINSHIP STRUCTURE

Migrants do not represent a random sample of the home community. Moreover, the selective nature of migration makes it impossible to reproduce the home community's kinship structure. Numerous studies have shown that, through time and space, migration is selective by age (Balán, Browning, and Jelin 1973; Portes and Bach 1985; Rodríguez 1987). The Totonicapán Maya in Houston are no exception. Approximately four-fifths of the men and women in my sample were under the age of thirty, and only 3 percent were over age forty. This concentration in the young-adult ages is a product of the pattern of selectivity and the fact that this population migrated to Houston relatively recently. Obviously, we would expect that as the group remains in Houston, there will be an aging in the population. We might also anticipate that once members of the community acquire permanent resident status through legalization, they may well petition for older and younger relatives to join them in the United States. Both processes would, in the long run, produce an age and sex structure among the Maya in Houston that more closely resembles that found in their home community.

For now, however, the concentration of young adults in the Maya community in Houston makes it impossible to reproduce the kinship structure from back home. The full panoply of extended kin, comprising the Maya patrilineal and patrilocal family groups (Wagley 1949), obviously cannot be reproduced in Houston. It is perhaps the parents who are missed most, since their absence implies a dual loss: as parents for the young migrants and as grandparents for their young children.

However, there is a concerted effort to compensate for this loss. Single mothers and parents migrating to Houston will often leave their children in Guatemala under the care of the grandparents. In some cases, U.S.-born children are being sent back to Guatemala to be raised. Leaving the children in the home country or sending them back meets several needs. Children are a solace to the grandparents at a time when two generations have been abruptly separated. In interviews conducted by Nestor Rodríguez and myself in 1989 and 1990 (interviews with aged members of migrant families in the home community), we found that fathers, mothers, and grandparents were not accepting of the long-term migration to Houston. Most had not seen their migrant sons and daughters for several years. To compensate for this loss, parents in Houston leave children with their grandparents in Guatemala. Leaving or sending children home is an important buffer against potential strain between migrants and their parents and is of some comfort to those parents.

Keeping children in Guatemala also allows for both parents to work full-time in the Houston labor market. Given that almost all young migrants in Houston are working, few extended kin or friends in the community are available to care for their children. Families who do have children in Houston are well established, and their children are of school age. It is not uncommon for a child to join his or her parents in Houston once the child has reached school age. Most young parents agree on the economic benefits of leaving their children in Guatemala. (In several cases U.S.-born children were sent back to Guatemala and then brought back to the community once the mother, a live-in domestic, "earned" the right to bring her own child into the employer's house.) On the whole, however, the Maya women prefer to have their children raised in Guatemala under the care of family and within a Maya culture. One young woman, who had not seen her child in three years, explained:

> It is very difficult for us. But we know she is safe and we will see her soon. We do it because we both have to work to pay for her education, but even if we could bring her I don't think we would, at least not yet. Her grandmother needs her and, most important, we want her to be brought up in Guatemala in an indígena community with strong values and good fresh air. We would be very worried if she lived here. I wouldn't know how to care for her. It takes all our time just to care for ourselves and send our family enough money to care for her. When we are more settled, perhaps she will join us. [Her child, Nancy, joined them in Houston two years later.]

Migrant parents who have left their children in Guatemala make every effort to maintain close ties with kin in the home community.

Given the vulnerability of migrants who do not have access to the varied resources normally provided by the kinship network in Guatemala, the Maya host community in Houston must, to a degree, act as a substitute. "Few strangers exist in the community," and this enhances the possibility for such support. Recall how friends and kin in the community responded to the widow of the young migrant who unexpectedly died.

Another example of unified community support emerged when two young men were picked up by the INS and transported to a detention center in southern Texas. After several weeks of unsuccessfully soliciting lawyers for assistance, the community drew on its own resources and produced the necessary dollars to post bail for the young men.

𝍎 RECRUITMENT NETWORKS AND THE JOURNEY

Kin and friendship networks quickly broadcast the arrival of newcomers throughout the community. Unlike the earliest migrants, who had few social ties to draw upon once in Houston, recent migrants have at their disposal a large number of kith and kin. These connections, which Browning and Rodríguez (1985) refer to as "social capital," provide tremendous assistance in the initial settlement of the newcomer.

Sponsoring households in Houston provide room, board, transportation, and sometimes even a job for most newcomers. Typically, the Houston contact is a brother, cousin, or brother-in-law. Usually, it seems, it is a male who arranges for the migration. This can partially be explained by the pattern of gender selectivity of earlier migration streams, the higher social and financial costs of female migration, and the more developed male job networks in the receiving community. I will elaborate on this last aspect in a section on work patterns, below.

Although male pioneers settled the community, an increasing number of single women have been arriving in recent years to join sisters, aunts, and sisters-in-law in Houston. In fact, current streams include equal numbers of women and men. The male migrants usually travel to Houston in small groups. In most cases, they travel by bus to Mexico and then hire a "coyote" to take them across the U.S.-Mexico border. The average cost of the trip is about five hundred dollars.

It is much more difficult for women to make the journey. The social and economic costs of the trip to Houston are higher for women than for men. Also, for obvious reasons, women are reluctant to travel alone or only with other women. While we rely on the news media to alert us to the increasing incidence of rape among undocumented women traveling north, the women learn about it from the rape victims themselves. Men are reluctant to travel with women because it is "harder when they are along."

Consequently, the female migrant must rely on two coyotes to get to Houston: one to take her through the highlands and across the Guatemalan-Mexican border; the other to take her through Mexico and across the U.S.-Mexico border. A friend or relative from the Houston community meets her once she has crossed the border into the United States. On average, women paid approximately twelve hundred dollars in coyote fees for the trip to the United States. Lidia describe the procedure for women.

> My family gave three hundred dollars to the coyote in Guate before I left. Some of this money was sent to Guate by my brother and cousin who live here in Houston. The coyote was also from Totonicapán. He made plans with a Mexican to pick me up in Chiapas [southern Mexico]. The Mexican took me across the U.S-Mexico border. It took me about three days. He was also bringing others—Mexicans—here. I've paid some back to the coyote. About another four hundred dollars. So I still owe him about five hundred dollars. [I then asked Lidia how and when she paid him.] He lives in Houston, not far from here. I pay him on a monthly basis.

I accompanied Lidia when she went to make her final payment. The coyote, a young Mexican, was noticeably nervous about my presence but could do little about it. When Lidia handed over the final payment of one hundred dollars, he returned to her a manila envelope containing her passport and all her other identification. According to Lidia, the rule of thumb is that the coyote keeps all identification papers until the final payment is made, thereby leaving the migrant truly undocumented, both in the United States and in Guatemala.

⚕ LIVING ARRANGEMENTS

Living arrangements in Houston are closely related to settlement stages (Rodríguez 1987), gender, and marital status. Once in Houston, the newcomer (male or female) becomes part of a new and rather heterogeneous living arrangement, one that departs significantly from the extended kin structure found in households in the home community. These household configurations may include multifamilies, combinations of kin, and nonrelated Maya boarders. Moreover, the composition shifts constantly as newcomers arrive and more-settled migrants move into new household arrangements. During the initial settlement stage, the households are large and diverse in composition, maximizing the migrant's limited financial resources. Unlike many other arriving migrants who may have no social resources in Houston (Rodríguez 1987), the newcomer Maya moves directly into a sponsoring household in the community, which provides room, board and, usually, access to employers. The presence of many San Pedro friends and kin in Houston makes the initial settling-in process relatively easy for the newcomer.

In stage two the migrant goes about the business of securing a job in order to raise his or her low level of financial resources. Getting a job can involve a considerable adjustment in living arrangements. For example, the male newcomer may move into a second household where established coworkers with cars reside. Access to a higher level of social resources, especially for the purpose of improving his employment status, may also spur the move into a second household. Often, such a move involves leaving family or kin and becoming a boarder.

Reaching the second settlement stage takes longer for the female newcomer and involves dramatic shifts in living arrangements. Since the job networks for females are not as resourceful as those for men (this differential will be explicitly described in the following section on job networks), women usually spend more time in the household of initial settlement. Once a live-in domestic position is located, the female migrant becomes part of two households: during the week, she resides in the employer's household; on the weekend, she returns to live among fellow Maya. For some of the female Maya, the second stage involves leaving the Maya household entirely. More affluent employers usually provide separate living arrangements for live-in domestics. A detached garage apartment located behind the main house of the employer becomes a second home for many of the women arriving in the community. The financial benefits of this arrangement are obvious: migrant women can avoid paying rent in the Maya household and can pay off their debt to the coyote at a faster rate.

Once a migrant has achieved a level of financial security and job stability, he or she often finds a new and better job. The ensuing improvement in the migrant's economic situation may motivate a change into a third household (Rodríguez 1987; Rodríguez and Hagan 1991). At this stage, the single-male migrant may move into a less-crowded household. Couples, including but not limited to husbands and wives, may make a variety of changes in their living arrangements. Some may move out of a multiple-family household to form a separate and smaller household. This change usually involves bringing along one or two immediate-family members or other relatives to join them, since financial pooling is still required where the wife is working as a live-in domestic. Husbands occasionally join their wives at their place of employment, if the quality of the detached house at the employer's is better than that found in the community and if the employer is agreeable. This is a desirable household arrangement for many young couples: not only does it allow them live together and to save rent money, but it also makes it possible for the men to earn extra money by doing chores for the employer (e.g., washing the cars, mowing the lawn). The single woman may also change her living arrangement, once her economic situation has improved. She may move out of the employer's household and back into the community on a full-time basis if she has made the transition to a day domestic. Another adjustment, when she can afford to pay weekend rent at the Maya household, may involve moving from full-time residency in the employer's home to a dual living arrangement. Most women will opt for these changes if they have the financial resources, since it allows them to spend more time in the community.

Maya living arrangements have several implications for two interrelated dimensions of community formation: 1. reproduction of Maya cultural practices and 2. reproduction of the gender-normative structure found back in Guatemala. Women occupy a central role in the reproduction of Maya culture with respect to maintaining religious practices, uniting community members through regular preparation of traditional foods, organizing community events, transmitting the Quiché language to the children, and preserving Maya identity by wearing the huipil and corte. The dual living arrangement, however, limits their role as reproducers of Maya culture by restricting their participation in the community to weekends and some weekday evenings at the community church.

The absence of parents from the Maya households, and from the community in general, challenges another dimension of community formation—the Maya normative structure. Without the watchful eyes of parents and other elderly kin, many singles in the community are likely to deviate from the behavioral norms that prevail back home. For example, it is not unusual to come across unmarried couples living together, couples separating because of extramarital relations, and cases of domestic violence.

It took me a long time to gain access to those few women

who would speak about these issues. Consequently, it is difficult to be precise as to the extent of these behaviors in the community; for to the outside observer's eye, relations seem harmonious. My female informants expressed mixed feelings about absent parents and the changing norms governing gender relations. The following comments come from conversations that occurred shortly after I learned that one of my principal informants had been badly beaten by her husband. One young woman responded to my concern:

> Yes, we all know he beats her. I feel for her, but I won't go to that apartment anymore because he drinks so much. I don't know her very well because she's from Alajuela [a cantón located just outside of San Pedro]. I know him though, and I also know that if he were in Guate he would never get away with it. His parents would ask him to leave the house because of the shame it would bring. But it probably wouldn't happen in Guate, because he wouldn't be drinking so much. I haven't had any problems with the men here. I like the freedom I have here. I can go out to parties, I can go out with men alone, I know it won't be like this if I go home. I want to go back, but the hardest thing will be acting like before, like my parents will expect. I wish they were here to understand how I am changing and to help with the problems some of us are having.

Another young woman, Teresa, who recently separated from her husband, had this to say:

> Jaime [her husband] came to Houston two years before me. I stayed in Guate with my children and his parents. I was very happy about coming to see him, even though I had to leave my children in Guate. I was here two days before I heard that he was with another woman all that time. This kind of thing happens. Not that much, but it

happens when we separate and our parents are not here to help. We arrive here and the men have changed. They are drinking, seeing other women, and sometimes even hit us. Most of the time, once the wife is here, he calms down a bit. But you know why? Because she calls his parents or at least threatens to. I am not going back to him. Most women stay with them and work things out with help from parents back home. I don't want to be with him, and I don't want to upset my family. It's hard because even though we were dependent on our parents back home, we are more dependent on the men here. We don't have our own homes. I move into their house on the weekend. [Teresa's father did try to come to Houston to speak with her husband. He was apprehended at the border, however. Six months later she moved back with her husband.]

Although many of the women enjoy discovering their new freedom, as their comments indicate, they also recognize the social and cultural costs of not having parents around. Equally interesting is the way some of the Maya men have interpreted and responded to the changing behavior of the Maya women in Houston. Carlos, a twenty-six-year-old who is unmarried and a practicing Protestant, spoke to the issue of marrying a Maya woman in the Houston community:

I wouldn't marry an Maya woman from Houston because they are too open and free now. They go out at night and dance and sometimes even drink beer. It is against the church and against their parents' wishes. When I get married, I will do it in Guate and bring her back with me.

When I related these comments to two of my female informants, they laughed, and one responded as follows:

They are not all like that, but some men want to control us like they did back home. It's different now, because we are making our own money and our parents are not here. Some of the men are just mad because some women say no and are dating men not in the community, like Mexicans and Salvadorans they meet at Santa María [a fictitious name for the Catholic church attended by the practicing Catholics in the community].

My findings suggest that three major features of the migration experience place a strain on traditional relations between men and women in the community, and consequently challenge community formation. First of all, the separation of couples, resulting from the earlier arrival of the male spouse, places a strain on relationships within the household. Second, the absence of parents or other aged persons leads to the transformation of traditional norms. Third, women are employed for the first time and this poses contradictions in the female settlement experience. On the one hand, they enjoy the freedom and independence associated with having their own job. On the other hand, they feel more dependent on men because of their marginal presence in the community, resulting from having to live in their employer's household. They return to the Maya neighborhood on the weekend, during which time they depend on housing and transportation from one or more of the men in the community. Additional issues contributing to the different settlement experience of women will be examined below.

ᵻᵻ JOB NETWORKS AND THE WORK EXPERIENCE

An important function of a well-developed community structure is its ability to provide arriving immigrants with sufficient social networks to find employment. Our findings (Rodríguez and Hagan, 1989) show that, while all the Maya

TABLE 4

Occupational Distribution by Gender

	MEN		WOMEN		TOTAL	
	%	NO.	%	NO.	%	NO.
Manager	2.3	1	—	—	1.3	1
Maintenance/stock worker	83.7	36	3.1	1	49.3	37
Mechanic	2.3	1	—	—	1.3	1
Baker	4.6	2	—	—	2.7	2
Cook	2.3	1	—	—	1.3	1
Domestic	—	—	96.9	31	41.3	31
Day laborer	4.6	2	—	—	2.7	2
TOTAL	99.8	43	100.0	32	99.9	75

NOTE: Total number exceeds the number of individuals in the sample where those with two occupations are counted twice

use networks to locate jobs, these networks operate different-ly for men and women. As Table 4 shows, some five-sixths of the men in my sample are employed as maintenance or stock workers in the same retail supermarket chain where Juan has been working since his arrival in Houston. Unlike many other undocumented immigrant workers in Houston, who are found in a variety of industries (e.g., service, construction) and informal work arrangements (e.g., temporary yard work), the Maya men dominate the maintenance department of one large and expanding retail chain, which has many outlets scattered throughout the greater Houston area. Their con-centration in this one firm can be explained by the Maya's well-developed social networks and the immigrants' control of the employment process. Arriving undocumented Maya are restricted to the use of social-networks to gain access to jobs. All newly arrived Maya men obtain jobs through friends, relatives, and other connections who are already employed in these workplaces.

The social network performs two important functions for

the new, undocumented worker to obtain a job. First, friends, relatives, and others in the social network inform the prospective worker of the availability of a job. If the prospective worker is still in Central America, this function is carried out via a phone call or letter, or by sending a message with a migrant who is returning to Central America.

Second, a member of the sponsoring social network introduces the new worker to the employer. This is a critical function in the case of the retail chain, where a new immigrant worker will not be hired unless he is recommended by another immigrant worker, preferably by the *encargado* (informal supervisor of the Maya workers in the retail chain). The Maya job networks control the information about the availability of new jobs. As Juan, the former encargado, reported, "the workers know even before employers when a job opening will occur because they [the maintenance/stock workers] know when a worker plans to quit [and return home] or temporarily leave [and return home for a visit] or ask for a job in another department or another store." Juan then went on to describe the immigrants' control of the maintenance jobs:

> It is difficult for them [the managers] to do it [i.e., hire a nonimmigrant worker for a maintenance job] because we [the immigrant maintenance workers] do not let it happen. We know when a worker is going to ask to move up [to another department], and we ourselves are already deciding who to bring in [as a replacement]. That is, we ourselves know when someone is going to move or leave, even though the store managers do not yet know. They themselves [the workers] say, "I want to move up and I want to talk with them [the store managers] if they will allow me." So one [the encargado] knows then. One [the encargado] talks to the manager and says, "You know he is going to move up, and [therefore] I need another worker." And I bring him one [a new worker]. And so

> there is no time [for managers] to make an announce-
> ment about a job opening. That is why another
> [nonimmigrant] worker cannot enter there [the mainte-
> nance department]. It is not because they [the managers]
> do not want him. It is because we know when someone is
> going to leave [the maintenance department] and, though
> the managers do not know, we already have a person
> ready [for the vacated maintenance job].

It is hard to envision another employment situation that
would allow workers in the maintenance department so much
control of the hiring process. This social control has become
a social comfort. Availing themselves of the protection of
encargados in the work-related social networks, some workers miss several days of work a month without fear of being
reported to the store managers. During the summer season,
workers negotiate among themselves about who goes on va-
cation during their hometown's yearly fiesta. In effect, the
Maya have reorganized the employment process according to
the social and cultural principles that exist back home in
Guatemala (Rodríguez 1989b; Hagan 1989).

Employers see the Maya as superior workers (responsible,
hardworking, etc.) who provide a self-regulating labor supply.
The workers also have a high degree of loyalty to the firm; it
has been their economic security since their arrival, and for
the most part, they have prospered. Indeed, inquiries show
that not only are there no plans to leave the firm but that the
workers look forward to locating jobs for relatives and friends
in new stores as they open.

The female workers in the community are also concentrated in one industry and one job type. As Table 4 shows, all
but one of the women in the sample are employed as domestics, and the majority of these positions are as live-in domestics. Women also use social network strategies to gain access
to jobs. Three types of social networks direct domestics to

individual households: employee networks; employer networks; and employer-employee networks. On occasion, employers and employees may approach an intermediary, such as myself, for assistance.

Despite the fact that both the Maya men and women use social networks to locate work, the Maya men fare better than the Maya women in Houston's labor market. This difference can be attributed to several social and structural factors, including the different dynamics of women's and men's job networks and the size and growth of the workplaces and industries in which they are incorporated.

First, with an extensive array of established male networks (within and outside of the workplace), recently arrived Maya men enjoy almost immediate access to jobs. Indeed, some of the men are recruited (often through the encargado) while still in Guatemala. Moreover, the men are employed in a fast-growing industry which naturally provides abundant employment slots. For example, when a new supermarket opens, so do several dozen jobs. Additionally, while most starting male workers earn the minimum wage, over time they experience both increases in wages and some mobility within the workplace.

The newcomer women face very different employment prospects. In contrast to the men, they encounter smaller and, thus, less resourceful networks. Newcomer women almost exclusively rely on more established domestics in the community to locate jobs. These women usually live at the workplace and, thus, have less time and opportunity to interact with newcomers and to assist them in finding work. Moreover, employment is based on a small workplace (i.e., one private home needing one worker) in an unpredictable industry. This means that women wait longer than men to locate jobs because each newcomer woman has to locate a separate employer, while teams of men are hired by one employer. Additionally, because of the nonregulated character of the domestic industry, most women are paid in cash on a weekly basis, usually earning far below the minimum wage. Moreover, the move from live-in to day domestic work (where earnings are greater) is a long process and usually requires command of English and the purchase of a car.

Employers—whether of domestics or of maintenance workers—comment on the desirability of the Maya, but the hiring process for the domestics is more arbitrary. Employers of Maya domestics typically base their decision on the personal characteristics and skills of the individual (e.g., physical appearance, English skills). This means, of course, that the Maya women must be present to be employed. Not so with the men, who have an encargado to negotiate prospective employment.

Undocumented Guatemalan women are seen as "more passive," "more loyal," and "less hostile" than Mexicans and African-Americans. The female employers I interviewed are influenced by all sorts of stereotypes. Newcomer immigrants are seen as less trouble, while established immigrant groups, such as Mexicans, are viewed as drinking too much or spending too much time with their boyfriends. Different stereotypes are applied to the African-American female workers, who, many employers believe "will rob them blind." One employer responded, when I asked why she preferred Guatemalan Maya workers:

> Well, I've had many girls clean my house, both Salvadorans and Mexicans. I now have a Guatemalan living here who cleans the house and cares for my daughter. And there's a difference. First, I feel the Guatemalan girl is more responsible with the children. She spends more time playing with the child and never lets her out of her sight. She is also very respectful of me and doesn't abuse the house like other maids have. Mexicans are always on the phone, having guys over when you're out, and eating

things without asking. It's not just me. Even my friends agree. Mexicans are just too aggressive, too demanding. The Guatemalans are more loyal and less likely to show their temper. They make better workers.

The domestic's degree of loyalty to her employer and level of enthusiasm toward her work changes with the amount of time spent on the job. New workers adorn their bedroom walls (in the immigrant apartment) with pictures of the family for whom they work; they praise them for their kindness. More established workers are somewhat critical of their situation and express resentment about working long, unpredictable hours and about being restricted to the employer's house. All domestics comment on the isolation from the community and on the loneliness they feel in their jobs.

Unlike their male counterparts, who are often found working alongside one another or pooling rides to work on a daily basis, female members of the community find such interaction limited by the very nature of their work. The typical scenario for a female in the community involves working from Monday to Saturday in the employer's household and returning to the community on Sundays. Without an effective, citywide mass-transportation system, most domestics are literally trapped in their employer's home for the entire work week.

Rafaela is a recent arrival to the community. Within several weeks of her arrival, her sister's employer had located a job for Rafaela as a live-in domestic. I met Rafaela shortly after she had landed this job. She complained about the loneliness and isolation. She had yet to see many of her friends from back home, although she knew where they were living in Houston. Basically, she said, there "just isn't time [to interact] because of work." Employed six days a week, she has only one free day—Sunday—to visit the community. Since her arrival, she has spent most Sundays with her two sisters, who are also live-in domestics and who work in the same neighborhood where she is employed. None of the sisters has a car, and so they are forced to rely on men in the community for transport. Already Rafaela is considering going back home unless she can change her employment situation. What she wants most is to work as a day domestic because of "the greater freedom involved." When I asked her what she meant by freedom, she said: "the freedom to live among the community, not away from it."

The work experience limits Rafaela and most females in the community to interacting solely with their employer during the week. If they are lucky, they will have an opportunity to reestablish ties with community members on weekends. Consequently, Maya women, because of their particular work conditions, settle into a limited network structure. Men, in contrast, are embedded in more social networks, enabling them to take advantage of the resources and information passed via these abundant networks.

Only three of the approximately thirty immigrants who approached me for assistance in preparing the visa application for the 1988 lottery were women. Yet it is the women in the community who most needed to apply for the visas, as the majority of them did not participate in IRCA. My research found that the different conditions under which men and women work lead to the development of more restricted networks for women, especially as the settlement period grows.

FORMATION OF COMMUNITY ORGANIZATIONS

The Community Church

The "community church" performs important functions in the formation and reproduction of the Maya community. Above all, it provides for regular interaction among the members of the community. Newcomers are able to meet some of the established community members at the weekly services. Women separated from the community during the week have an opportunity to see family and friends during the weekend nights when special services and reunions occur. Resources are shared; information is passed among members. At the church, the community is united in its common belief system.

The church, La Iglesia de Dios, is a Protestant church espousing an evangelical doctrine. Although located miles away from the members' residences, the church is a source of continual pride and promotes solidarity among community members. It is the oldest and most important religious institution bonding the Totonicapán Maya in Houston. When the immigrants first started attending the Protestant church in the early 1980s, it was approximately 80 percent Mexican and 20 percent Guatemalan and had a Mexican pastor. As Maya membership grew, so did tensions between the two immigrant groups. The Maya felt that the services were not "structured enough" and that the Mexican parishioners were too "informal." When asked for more specificity, they commented on how the Mexican women wore what the Maya considered to be inappropriate clothing to services (e.g., slacks, tight sweaters). By the mid-eighties the Guatemalan membership exceeded Mexican membership. At that point, the Mexicans decided to start a new church, and the existing church was left to the Maya parishioners. One of the first actions they took was to try to locate and bring in a Guatemalan pastor. When that failed, they settled on a Puerto Rican pastor. Today, all the parishioners are Maya migrants from the Department of Totonicapán.

The church provides several opportunities for community interaction. These include Sunday and Wednesday services which all members attend; a Saturday Bible-reading session in which only the women and their daughters participate; and a *culto de hogar*, which brings members to one another's homes on Tuesday evenings to read the Bible and discuss ways in which its teachings can be applied to improve the lives of family and community members.

The Totonicapán Maya bear the financial costs of maintaining the community church, including the rent of the building and the charges for electricity. Funds to maintain the church were initially generated through monthly fundraising events. Usually about thirty women work together in one household, preparing tamales to sell to immigrant households within the community. As the number of women in the community swells, however, it becomes increasingly difficult to bring together so many women at the same time. Consequently, it is now the responsibility of one woman each month to make the tamales. Even nonchurchgoers know who is preparing tamales for any given month, and the tamales are sold to all community members, regardless of religious affiliation.

Not all immigrants in the community are members of the community church, and of those who do participate in church activities, not all do so with the same fervor. Approximately 60 percent of the Totonicapán immigrants are members of this particular Protestant church. The remaining immigrants either attend the Catholic church (Santa María) located near their residence or they do not practice any religion.

Being a member or not being a member of the community church appears to be the strongest source of dissension within the community. In the initial stages of settlement, the majority of newcomers were active in the church, but many of the immigrants have commented that over time they withdrew from the church because they found the moral sanctions too rigid (e.g., no dancing or drinking). Some of those who left the community church began attending Santa María because it provided a variety of activities for single members in the community (e.g., dances and Bible-study groups).

While full participation in the community church strength-

A father joins his children at a wedding ceremony in the
Houston community church

ens a formal network among active churchgoers and creates
an additional feeling of community for a select portion of the
community, all immigrants from Totonicapán, regardless of
religious identity, are indirectly affected by the social and
cultural forces of the Protestant church. Many marriages,
quinceañeras, and other major life-cycle events are celebrat-
ed in this church, and many community members attend such
events. Thus, even among nonchurchgoers, the Protestant
church serves to unite the community for important life-
cycle events. In contrast, the Catholic church, which is
frequented by many newcomer and established-resident
groups, provides an opportunity for interaction with non-
Maya churchgoers.

The Community Soccer Club

A second organization that functions to circulate information within the Maya community and that provides for regular social interaction is the community soccer club. In the

early days of their immigration, the Maya men met informally to play soccer. As more migrants came to Houston, interest grew in developing a league. By the early 1980s, three Totonicapán soccer teams constituted the second community-developed organization in Houston. In a conscious effort to maintain group solidarity, the Maya teams avoid playing one another. Competing with other immigrant soccer teams on a weekly basis, the Totonicapán soccer club functions as a social organization; most men in the community have participated at one time or another since their arrival. Interest in soccer peaked during the mid-1980s when one of the teams won a league championship; by 1986, however, interest had dwindled to only one active team, and it subsequently withdrew from local tournaments.

Several reasons are given by the Maya for the decreasing participation. First of all, some key players returned to Guatemala in 1986 because of the anticipated repercussions of IRCA. In addition, the team goalie was seriously injured.

The Houston San Pedro soccer team.

The Houston migrants' soccer team plays the San Pedro team at San Pedro.

Moreover, there is a lack of support from other community members, especially the women. Initially, women came out in substantial numbers to cheer on the home team. According to the women, however, it is extremely difficult to support the team on a regular basis because of the dual demands of work and church and the lack of transportation. Many women are busy with other activities on the weekends when the games take place. Almost 40 percent of the women work on Saturdays, and an even greater proportion spend Sunday afternoons at the community church. A really successful club requires the support of fans from the community, and the San Pedro teams have not been able to generate this support. Consequently, while the soccer club represents a social organization in which all indígenas can participate, it functions to reunite only the males in the community. At the soccer field, new male arrivals are welcomed to Houston, job contacts are made, and news is shared.

*Carmen records festivities in San Pedro for
the Houston community.*

The soccer club has met many community needs. Most
important, the club has served as a base for generating funds
for the larger Maya community. On one occasion, money was
raised to cover medical bills for an injured player. On another, team members were instrumental in the organization of a
fund-raising campaign to help a widow in the community
who had just lost her husband to illness. Team members went
from household to household to gather sufficient funds to
transport the body back home to Guatemala and to cover the
funeral costs in San Pedro. The soccer club also assists in the
process of community reproduction back home. Money sent
by the soccer teams has paid for part of the expenses of the

annual San Pedro fiesta. While the fiesta system has not been reproduced in Houston, it is maintained back home partly through funds raised by the soccer club in Houston.

IN PART ONE OF THIS BOOK, we have come to know something about the formation of a Maya community in Houston and about the settlement experiences of its members. Sharing a community of origin, along with an ability to transfer and reproduce cultural symbols from the home community, has clearly facilitated the formation of a Maya community in Houston. For recent Maya arrivals, the costs of settlement are eased by the existence of a well-developed community structure in Houston. This structure, characterized by multiple and overlapping social networks, provides a variety of social resources to the Maya newcomer.

The settlement experience of men and women is similar, yet different. While both men and women use networks to find housing, locate jobs, and ease in the overall settlement process, women's networks are fewer in number and weaker in nature. This difference explains the longer time it takes for women to find work. The impact of these gendered job networks on opportunities to legalize will be addressed in Part Two.

THE JOURNEY THROUGH LEGALIZATION

THE SOCIAL PROCESS OF BECOMING LEGAL

THEIR STORIES ALL BEGAN THE SAME. THEY WERE YOUNG, single, and living in a village that offered little in the way of economic opportunity. In 1984, Julia and Miguel each made the decision to follow a dream, designed and developed by so many of their friends and kin from the village of San Pedro— to go to Houston, where there is a daughter community to receive them and an opportunity to work. While Julia and Miguel agree that the primary factor motivating their migration was work, they expressed different reasons for seeking jobs here. Whereas Miguel said that he came for more secure work and higher wages to supplement the family's tailoring business, Julia came to earn enough money to get an education for her child, who was to stay in Guatemala under the care of Julia's mother. Once they achieved these goals, both Julia and Miguel intended to return home to San Pedro, Totonicapán. In Houston, they relied on the assistance of friends and kin already living there to find jobs. Miguel joined the ranks of many of his friends and relatives working in a local retail supermarket chain. Julia found part-time day work as a domestic, the typical employment track for the women of the community.

Though their stories may have begun the same, today their lives and plans for the future are quite different. Having gone through the legalization program, Miguel is now a permanent U.S. resident. Legal status has allowed him to make his first trip home to Guatemala since his arrival in Houston over four years ago, and he is planning another trip for sometime this summer. He is currently learning English at the high school in his neighborhood and is expressing doubts about returning home permanently. As Miguel says:

> Legal status has given me, for the first time, a sense of security in this country. Though I know life will not be easy for me here, the opportunities I dreamed of back home now have the chance to become reality.

Julia, on the other hand, was unable to secure the necessary documentation to legalize her status. Longing to see her child again, she recently scraped together her meager savings and made arrangements with a "coyote" to have her son brought to Houston. The bulk of her next six months' salary will be handed over to the coyote for his services. Today, she expresses fear and uncertainty when she talks about her future in the United States:

> If only I had been able to get amnesty like others in the community—things would be different—at least I would have something to look forward to like going to visit my mother or finding full-time work in Houston.

At the time of this writing, Julia remains uncertain regarding her future plans. There is no way for her to make a decision about returning to Guatemala or staying in Houston. She lives day to day, hand to mouth, and there is little hope for change in this precarious situation so long as she remains part of the "new undocumented"—an adverse consequence of

IRCA. Julia now expresses a desire to one day marry her current live-in boyfriend, a fellow Maya, who has legal status. If they marry, she reasons, she and her child can eventually petition for legal status. She is aware of this new dimension of dependence on a man who has, in fact, physically and emotionally abused her in the past. She also realizes, however, that this is an emerging reality—one facing several of the remaining undocumented women in the community.

In this chapter we will look at the legalization program from the perspective of the immigrant community. For the Maya in Houston, the meaning of legalization was interpreted against the backdrop of the immigrants' preexisting agendas, and successful participation in the program was largely influenced by the community's ability to meet those agendas. To understand this perspective, we need to understand the workings of IRCA at the national level and at the level of program implementation and performance in Houston. I will limit this preliminary discussion, however, to a brief overview so that we may then experience the legalization process as it was viewed and interpreted by the Totonicapán Maya in Houston. The legalization journey takes the immigrant through several stages: 1. planning and decision making; 2. collecting documentation; and 3. adjudicating for temporary residence. Thus, the present chapter follows the temporal dimension of the program and examines the social context of the stages constituting the legalization process.

♟ AN OVERVIEW OF IRCA

Historically, U.S. immigration policy has been charged with framing the parameters for legal immigration, and the major periods of immigration reform have either restricted or expanded the conditions under which people migrate legally to the United States. The Immigration Reform and Control Act of 1986 departs dramatically from this historical pattern by being the first piece of legislation to attack undocumented migration directly.

Major reforms in immigration policy in 1965 laid the foundation for increases in the volume of immigration (legal as well as undocumented) to the United States. Passage of the 1965 amendments to the Immigration and Nationality Act of 1952 dismantled the national-origin quotas that had been in effect since the 1920s and gave priority to family reunification as the basis for immigrant admission. These amendments led to levels of immigration comparable only to the peak immigration years of the twenties. At the same time, the amendments placed new restrictions on the number of Western Hemisphere immigrants, including immigrants from Mexico, at 120,000 visas per year. The year 1965 also marks the end of the Bracero Program, an agreement operated jointly by Mexico and the United States to provide temporary Mexican workers for the U.S. agricultural industry. With the termination of the Bracero Program, INS rates of apprehension and deportation of undocumented Mexicans increased dramatically.

Thus, it was the combined effect of family reunification policies and numerical restrictions, coupled with the termination of the Bracero Program, that generated the increase in undocumented Mexican immigration. As the number of undocumented immigrants entering the United States swelled over the ensuing decade, the U.S. public and their congressional leaders became increasingly concerned about the social and economic consequences of this influx, especially the perceived negative effects on employment opportunities for authorized workers. By the late 1970s, undocumented immigration came to be defined by lawmakers and citizens alike as a "social problem" to be reckoned with.

The Carter administration responded by establishing the

Select Commission on Immigration and Refugee Policy (SCIRP) in 1978; its mandate was to investigate all aspects of U.S. immigration policy. In its 1981 report, the sixteen-member commission concluded that the "most pressing" immigration issue was that of undocumented immigration. Two legislative approaches were recommended: employer sanctions and "amnesty" for undocumented workers (SCIRP 1981). The principal theme was articulated by Father Hesburgh, head of the commission, when he wrote that to keep the front door open we must close the back door, that is, to keep legal admissions, we must decrease illegal immigration (see Miller 1985:55).

The SCIRP report pushed the legislature into action. It had been thirty years since the House and Senate convened for joint hearings on immigration policy. From these joint hearings emerged a series of immigration reform bills, including the Immigration Reform and Control Act of 1982, cosponsored by Senator Alan Simpson of Wyoming and Representative Romano Mazzoli of Kentucky. The key provisions of the bill included employer sanctions for their undocumented workers and a legalization program. While the bill passed the Senate with ease in 1982, it failed in the House. The strongest congressional supporters of amnesty in the House and among lobbyists (e.g., advocacy groups, Hispanic groups) were also the strongest opponents to employer sanctions. Similarly, advocates of employer sanctions (e.g., organized labor) were strongly opposed to legalization (Baker 1990). The immigration debate was to struggle through several sessions of Congress until October 1986, when a series of compromises led to the passage of IRCA by the Ninety-ninth Congress. On November 6, 1986, IRCA was signed into law by Ronald Reagan.

IRCA's major objective—to curtail undocumented immigration to the United States—was expected to be accomplished by the complementary effects of it's two key provisions:

employer sanctions and legalization. Blended into IRCA, these two provisions reflect the struggle between the inclusionary (nation of immigrants) and exclusionary (border integrity) strands of political thought in U.S. immigration policy (Baker 1990; Hagan and Baker 1993). The cornerstone of IRCA, employer sanctions, represents the control measure of IRCA; it imposes penalties on employers who hire unauthorized workers. This, in effect, ended the thirty-four-year-old "Texas Proviso," which had exempted employers from legal culpability for employing unauthorized workers. The premise behind employer sanctions is that work is the primary factor drawing the undocumented to the United States and that by removing this incentive, incursions by undocumented workers can be reduced (Keely 1989).

The second major provision, legalization, represents the benefits side of IRCA; it provides two main paths to permanent U.S. residence: a one-shot general legalization program, for undocumented immigrants already living in the country, and a special agricultural-worker legalization program (SAW)[1]. Given the focus of this book—one urban community's experience with the legalization program—the following discussion is restricted to the first path, hereafter referred to as "amnesty," "the legalization program," or "legalization."[2]

Section 245 of IRCA defines the parameters for legalization eligibility and outlines the basic procedure for acquiring legal status. The statute permitted undocumented workers living in the United States since January 1, 1982, to regularize their status. Excluded under IRCA were people with criminal records or serious communicable diseases, people who were likely to become a public charge, and people who made fraudulent use of immigration documents. Applicants were required to provide, with documentation, evidence of unlawful entry into the United States before January 1, 1982, and proof of continuous unlawful residence thereafter (brief absences were permitted); they also had to demonstrate that they could be self-supporting. Filing fees were included ($185 per adult, $50 per child; or a $420 cap per nuclear family). In contrast to the employer sanctions provision, which was funded through the IRCA budget, the legalization program was funded entirely through applicant fees (Baker 1990).

Legalization involved a two-step process, including temporary resident status and permanent resident status. Eligible persons had a one-year window in which to apply. If approved, all applicants would go through an eighteen-month temporary residency stage, during which time they were authorized to work. At the end of the eighteen-month period, applicants would have one year in which to apply for permanent resident status. If they failed to apply for permanent resident status, their temporary resident status would revert to an undocumented status. The transition from temporary resident to permanent resident involved several additional requirements, including completion of an English/civics class or demonstration of English skills and knowledge of U.S. political history. Finally, applicants were barred from most public benefits throughout temporary residency and the first two years of permanent residency. Once permanent resident status was granted, the immigrant could sponsor a spouse and children for permanent residency. After five years of permanent residence, legalized immigrants were eligible for U.S. citizenship.

In addition to the 107 INS legalization offices established throughout the country to process applications, the INS also formed working relationships with hundreds of local voluntary agencies and community organizations to help recruit applicants and prepare their applications. Referred to as Qualified Designated Entities (QDEs) in IRCA statutory language, these agencies (churches, schools, etc.) served to maximize participation in the legalization program. It was believed that

QDEs would counter the adverse effects of the fear immigrant communities have of the INS. Their role was to act as a buffer between the immigrant population and the INS (Keely 1989). The QDEs were permitted to accept legalization applications and to assist applicants in acquiring and organizing the appropriate documentation. The QDE would then forward the completed applications to the INS, for which the QDE would receive fifteen dollars per application.

Not even IRCA's staunchest critics can deny the success of the legalization program: the numbers speak to it's success. The INS estimated the population eligible for legalization under the general amnesty program at between 1.3 and 2.6 million. By the time the program's office doors closed at midnight on May 3, 1988, applications for adjustment to legal status had been accepted from 1.7 million undocumented persons. The legalization program proved more successful than earlier critics had anticipated, and in a few locations it far exceeded preliminary projections (Meissner and Papademetriou 1988; Bean, Edmonston, and Passel 1990a). The U.S. legalization program was based partly on the programs of other countries, and it will probably go down in history as the single most ambitious and successful program, considering its size and the proportion of the estimated eligible population who have been legalized (Keely 1989).[3]

Yet, despite these observations, only a handful of studies have directly explored the social and political processes that led to high participation (Hagan and Baker 1993; Baker 1990; Meissner and Papademetriou 1988; North and Portz 1988). Moreover, the majority of these studies examine the implementation process and program participation from the perspective of the implementing agencies and institutions (e.g., local INS agencies, QDEs); only recently have studies addressed the role of the target group (immigrant communities) in explaining program participation (Hagan and Baker 1993).

⚟ LEGALIZATION IN HOUSTON

Houston INS officials had reason to brag that the twenty-nine-county Houston district had the "busiest" legalization center in the country (Houston Chronicle 1988). Indeed, the Houston office holds the distinction of processing more legalization applications than any other office in the country.[4] By the time the doors to the legalization office closed on May 3, 1988, no fewer than 113,870 applications for legalization had been filed in Houston, and of these, 99,592 were granted temporary resident status. The majority of Houston's legalization population comes from Mexico (66%), followed by Central America (25%). The remaining applicants come from other countries in the eastern and western hemisphere (INS 1992).

Several factors account for Houston's surprising numbers. For one thing, estimates of the population eligible for legalization were far too low. The U.S. Bureau of the Census, for example, estimated Houston's undocumented population in 1980 to be 51,956.[5] This low estimate (which points to the fundamental problem with estimates of the undocumented population—the fact that it is not possible to establish a base population from which to develop estimates) helped make Texas the only state to exceed the "high range" planning estimate of legalization turnout issued by INS immediately before implementation (Baker 1990).

The low estimates alone do not account for Houston's surprising numbers. Indeed, a number of studies have found that application rates have not been uniformly high in all states (Keely 1989; North and Portz 1989; Meissner and Papademetriou 1988; Baker 1990). Some states in the Northeast, for example, received applications at a rate well below expectations, while states in the Southwest received applications far exceeding expectations. Thus, New York City, with an estimated undocumented population of well over 500,000, received approximately 100,000 applications. This number is comparable to the number filed in Houston, which had a smaller undocumented immigrant community.

Immigration researchers who traced program implementation have offered several reasons for the regional variations. Among the many factors listed to explain successful program participation, the most frequently mentioned include 1. the aggressive nature of private publicity efforts (especially important, given that the formal public information effort fell short of its mission); 2. the active roles assumed by local INS regional and district managers; and 3. outreach programs, advocacy efforts, and court cases waged by community organizations, churches, and coalitions (Meissner and Papademetriou 1988; Baker 1990).

In Houston, all of these factors operated to enhance program participation. Moreover, implementation efforts were overwhelmingly directed toward reaching the largest of Houston's undocumented communities, the Hispanic community. Thus, it is important to note that the relative homogeneity of Houston's undocumented community, with respect to language and ethnicity, also contributed to the comparative ease with which these efforts reached the undocumented community.

Houston's newspapers and other news media organizations were extensive in their coverage of the legalization program. One of Houston's two leading newspapers, the *Houston Chronicle*, covered the legalization issue over the entire span of the program and alerted readers to changes in the development of the program as it was being implemented. Ethnic news media and papers, especially Spanish-language papers, television stations, and radio stations, also followed the legalization issue very closely. Indeed, Spanish-language television and radio stations covered the issue on a weekly, sometimes even daily basis.

Local INS officials were also very aggressive in selling legalization to Houston's immigrant community. The legalization office was located in a shopping center in a well-known Mexican American barrio, miles away from the INS investigating and enforcement office. Legalization personnel were hired from outside the agency as temporary employees, and the legalization director for the Houston district was brought in from another social service agency. Both the district director and the program director were Mexican American, as were many of the office staff who conducted the applicant interviews (Hagan and Baker 1993). According to local INS officials, the local director of the legalization program took the program "personally," holding "town meetings" in Hispanic neighborhoods, giving briefings, and appearing regularly on local television and radio talk shows.

Community-based organizations and local entrepreneurs, who had a history of servicing Houston's large immigrant population, also played a role in promoting high turnout. This group included the QDE network (twenty-four local entities in Houston), voluntary agencies with long-established ties to the immigrant community (e.g., churches), and those who viewed legalization as a profit-making opportunity (e.g., *notarios públicos* [notary publics] and private immigration attorneys) (Hagan and Baker 1993). Although QDEs did not file as many local applications as expected (20%), they, along with other local service groups and advocacy organizations, played a crucial role. In light of their low application rate, their important role in screening applicants and monitoring INS procedures could easily go unnoticed. Early in the program, local Catholic churches, acting as QDEs, made information available to their parishioners about program eligibility and filing requirements. Many prospective applicants went first to trusted QDEs for advice, and only then filed with INS. We found that QDEs were crucial in disseminating clear information locally and in facilitating the approval of applications (Hagan and Baker 1993).

Notarios benefited from the fact that "notary public"

status serves as a functional equivalent to legal counsel in Latin American countries. Many notarios sprang up overnight in Houston's barrios. There was considerable range in the fees notarios were charging for legalization assistance; some charged as little as fifteen dollars for an application, while others charged hundreds. Although the INS conferred legitimacy on some notaries through the "QDE" designation, as a group they were regarded with much skepticism by nonprofit organizations and immigration attorneys. Such skepticism was partially borne out, and INS prosecuted many notarios for immigration fraud (Baker 1990). On the other hand, without the relatively inexpensive fees charged by a number of notarios, some of the Maya would not have been able to seek legalization.

In general, studies of IRCA implementation have found a national pattern in which the legalization program became increasingly more inclusive as courts and advocacy groups pressured INS to relax eligibility restrictions (Baker 1990; Meissner and Papademetriou 1988). In Houston, we found that QDEs and other community-based organizations contributed to more program participation as they developed informal and formal linkages with the INS and ultimately reinterpreted their legalization role from administrative to activist (Hagan and Baker 1993). Local group agencies in Houston and elsewhere in the country recognized early the problems people were having in documenting their clandestine existence in the United States. They pressed local INS officials for a more liberal interpretation of the rules. In Houston, for example, a coalition of immigrant-servicing groups convened under an umbrella community task force to provide the immigrant and business communities with answers to questions about IRCA implementation.[6] The task force met regularly with INS, produced publicity materials to compensate for the slow development and arrival of INS-sponsored material, appeared on Spanish-language television and radio talk shows, and solicited public endorsements of rights from city officials. Where informal strategies fell short, these groups pressed ahead with lawsuits.

QDEs were active in filing several of the major class-action lawsuits that successfully challenged operational definitions of program regulations. As INS continued its losing streak in most of these court battles, reform was mandated that increasingly liberalized standards (Hagan and Baker 1993). Legal action, taken in Houston and throughout the nation, successfully resulted in the inclusion of applicant pools that had originally been excluded by program regulations: foreign students and persons who had overstayed their visitor visas (Ayuda, Inc. v. Meese 1988); undocumented immigrants who had returned to their communities of origin for a short period (Catholic Social Services v. Meese 1988); applicants turned down because they had received certain types of public assistance (Zambrano v. Meese 1988); and applicants who relied primarily on affidavits as documentation for eligibility (Loe v. Thornburgh 1989; Hiracheta v. Thornburgh 1989). What is important here is that many of these lawsuits were filed by QDEs, agencies originally as seen as partners with the INS in legalization implementation (Hagan and Baker 1993).

While the responses of these social actors certainly help to explain why legalization was so successful, they do not tell the whole story. We must now turn to those who were most affected by the program, yet least often heard. The immigrant communities were key players affecting the outcome of the legalization program. The Maya were far more than passive recipients of immigration policy: they perceived, interpreted, and ultimately acted upon the program. It is to their perceptions and actions that we now turn.

👥 **IMMIGRANT PERSPECTIVES**

Stage One: Decision Making and Planning

Mario, a twenty-four-year-old tailor and subsistence farmer from San Pedro, has lived in Houston since 1984. His case is typical of many of the Maya who came to Houston on a temporary basis, planning to stay just long enough to earn the necessary capital to invest back home. When I first interviewed Mario in late 1987, he had no intention of applying for legalization. When I asked if his reason was related to his eligibility (he had arrived after the January 1, 1982, cutoff date), he said no, claiming he knew "others in the community who were not eligible, yet still applied." I asked him, then, to explain why. He responded:

> It makes no sense to apply since I plan on returning home as soon as I earn enough money to buy an industrial sewing machine and finish the house I am having built in San Pedro. My family is there, and that is where I want to be.

Less than a month later I learned that Mario had indeed filed his application for legalization. When I asked him about his change in plans, he said:

> I haven't changed my mind. As I told you before, I plan on returning to Guatemala as soon as I have enough money. I am not interested in becoming a resident of this country and I don't expect them [INS] to give it [legal status] to me. I only applied for amnesty because of work authorization. I don't expect to get legal residency. I am buying more time to earn more money.

Even though Mario did not expect to be granted temporary resident status, as he was not entirely eligible, he took the detailed steps to prepare his documentation. Two months later, he received his temporary residency card. Some time later, I ran into Mario at the local high school where many in the Maya community were taking the required English classes to qualify for permanent residency. I now asked him if he was also studying English to prepare for the second stage of legalization—permanent residency. He told me, "I still am not planning to go that far, but who knows?" Several months later, Mario dropped by my apartment and asked for help in preparing his application file for permanent residency. When I asked why he had changed his mind again, he said:

> I never expected to get this far. Now that I have temporary residency and am learning English, it makes more sense to apply for permanent residency. But this doesn't mean I have any plans to become an American citizen. I still plan to return home.

With a bit more probing, I learned that Mario had a new girlfriend. He felt that because she was planning to apply for permanent residency, he should too. They were making plans to visit Guatemala together. Despite all the actions he has formally taken toward permanently settling in the United States, Mario still believes that he will return to Guatemala for good as soon as he has saved enough money.

Mario's words and actions depict the ambiguity of settlement, especially the shifting nature of migrant decision making. His decisions change with his attitudes, options, and social relations, all of which alter with time. To an onlooker, it may appear that Mario is becoming a permanent settler in the United States. To Mario, however, his actions are merely strategies to buy time and earn money that will enable him to return home permanently. The very nature of undocumented life—with its high degree of uncertainty and informality—discourages plans that go beyond securing the necessities of day-to-day living. Given this context, it is only natural that Mario should make two sets of plans, one to stay and one to return home. In doing so, he is keeping his options open in the context of rapidly changing circumstances.

Research on undocumented immigrant communities in the United States has focused on the complexity of the decision-making process as it relates to long-term settlement and acquisition of legal status (Massey et al. 1987; Portes and Curtis 1987; Portes and Truelove 1987). Pinpointing the actual processes influencing a migrant's decision to take the legal steps to settle in the United States has been extremely difficult because of the informal and temporal character of undocumented migration. Decisions are often based on a constantly changing set of attitudes, options, conditions, and relations in both the home community and host society. Therefore, it is not uncommon for a migrant to make frequent changes in his or her plans for settlement. The often informal—at times unpredictable—behavior among undocumented communities reflects the shifting nature of their decision-making processes in the face of a precarious legal status.

In their study of the social process of undocumented Mexican migration, Massey, Alarcón, Darand, and González (1987) found that although the probability of permanent settlement increases with time in the United States, rarely does the migrant take formal steps toward establishing long-term settlement plans. Indeed, the informal and clandestine nature of undocumented life, with its constant ambiguity, discourages the migrant from making or relying on long-term plans. These findings are consistent with the findings of the present study. For most Maya in the Houston community, decision making in regard to settlement is a continual process. In fact, I found that it can vary on a weekly, if not daily basis.

What is especially interesting about Mario's case is the complexity and sophistication of the decision-making process within the context of the formalized opportunity structure of IRCA. Even when legal vehicles are made available for purposes of settlement, decision-making processes remain fluid and continue to be influenced by personal as well as community transformations. Ultimately, immigrant options are left open and remain flexible until one is *forced* to make a decision. Nonetheless, through repeated interviewing at different points in time and in different contexts, I was able to distinguish patterns of community behavior and patterns of group motivation and expectation regarding legalization. It is to these emergent patterns that we now turn.

INITIAL COMMUNITY RESPONSES TO LEGALIZATION ～
When IRCA was signed into law on November 6, 1986, few INS officials, let alone potential immigrant applicants, understood the dynamics of the law, especially all the requirements for and implications of legalization. In fact, it was not until the program was implemented, the following May, that INS even made the regulations available to the public. During a discussion of the law in the early spring of 1987, Juan, the pioneer of the Maya community in Houston and one of the members legitimately eligible for legalization, presented the community's initial understanding of the effects of IRCA:

> We don't really understand the law completely, but we do know that only a few of us can apply for amnesty, and that most of us can expect to lose our jobs soon. We just don't know when. I am thinking of applying, but it will depend on whether I can get all the papers in order, it is going to be very difficult to find proof I have been working here all these years. Probably, most of us will be going home to Guate soon, maybe in the next few months when we no longer have work [referring to when employer sanctions were expected to be implemented.]

As Juan's comments illustrate, the community initially interpreted the letter of the law literally. Knowledge of IRCA was limited, but sufficient to anticipate that the twin blows of employer sanctions and legalization meant that most would lose their jobs and all but a handful in the community would be forced to leave the United States. The concern then became exactly when the law would have an impact on their lives in Houston. Consequently, during the first months following the passage of IRCA, the majority took a wait-and-see attitude: waiting to be fired from their jobs, at which time they would see about returning home.

Some potential migrants in the home communities, however, were unwilling to wait for the imminent passage of IRCA, let alone the possible ramifications of its implementation. They had watched, especially in recent years, an increasing number in their communities leave for Houston. The specter of IRCA appears to have galvanized their long-term plans into immediate action. Table 5, which includes the year of arrival of the study's seventy-four key informants, shows that migration to Houston from San Pedro increased steadily during the early- to mid-eighties, reflecting the establishment of a viable community in Houston. Immigration further escalated in 1986, just prior to the passage of IRCA, then declined dramatically in 1987, following the implementation of employer sanctions.[7]

The cloud of IRCA also precipitated immediate action among a few in the Houston community. In the early spring of 1987, the first significant wave of return migration to Totonicapán occurred. Fearing the effects of employer sanctions and INS crackdowns, over sixty in the larger Totonicapán community of a thousand returned to Guatemala. José, one of the many to make the trip, explained his early and strategic departure as a "way to beat the crowd home." I recall wondering, during this period of uncertainty and flux, whether the Maya community in Houston would survive another year under the cloud of IRCA, particularly the employer sanctions.

By the time the doors to the legalization office opened several months later on May 4, 1987, attitudes, perceptions, and understanding of IRCA had begun to change. Applica-

TABLE 5

Year of Arrival and Legal Status by Gender

	MEN		WOMEN		TOTAL	
	%	NO.	%	NO.	%	NO.
YEAR OF ARRIVAL						
Before January 1, 1982	19.0	8	6.2	2	13.5	10
1982	7.1	3	6.2	2	6.7	5
1983	7.1	3	6.2	2	6.7	5
1984	11.9	5	9.4	3	10.8	8
1985	26.2	11	18.7	6	23.0	17
1986	19.0	8	34.4	11	25.7	19
1987	—	—	3.1	1	1.3	1
1988	9.5	4	6.2	2	8.1	6
January–April 1989	—	—	9.4	3	4.0	3
TOTAL	99.8	42	99.8	32	99.8	74
LEGAL STATUS						
Legalization program	76.2	32	28.1	9	55.4	41
Political asylum applicant	2.4	1	—	—	1.3	1
Permanent resident or visa holder	7.1	3	—	—	4.1	3
Undocumented	14.3	6	71.9	23	39.2	29
TOTAL	100.0	42	100.0	32	100.0	74

tions were being prepared by several of the men in the community who were eligible for the program. This first group of community applicants took the process very seriously. They spent weeks meticulously gathering the necessary documentation and insisted on securing a lawyer to handle their cases. As others in the community observed the actions of these men, they learned "how it was done." The fear of employer sanctions was being replaced with a heightened interest in legalization. By the time these men filed their applications, in late June 1987, the idea of pursuing legalization had become a wide-ly discussed topic within the community.

The community waited. When the first group of applicants received their temporary residence cards, word of their success spread quickly. Others in the community who qualified for legalization responded by preparing their files. As those in the community who did not qualify watched the experiences of those who did, they expressed mild astonishment at the looseness with which applicants were being screened by INS. Some went so far as to compare the application process to "lotteries" back home. It was now September 1987, and employer sanctions had been in effect for several months. None of the Maya had lost their jobs; several of the women had changed jobs without difficulty; and a handful of the sixty who had left for Guatemala had already returned to Houston. Then events moved in an unforeseen direction.

Immigrants began to take the initiative. César and Andrés, young single men in the community who did not qualify for legalization, nonetheless filed their applications. Moreover, they passed their first interviews with INS. Within several weeks, they received their work authorization cards and were notified that their residence status would be determined by the regional office within six months. It took less than a week for word to spread throughout the community concerning the success of the two men. Information about how they had managed to secure the required documentation for their petitions began to circulate within the community.

Community social networks were instrumental in circulating information about the short-term benefits of applying for legalization (viz., authorization to work) and about the inner workings of the application process. "How to do it" became a widely discussed topic among coworkers, at soccer matches, and within households in the apartment complexes. Social networks provided community members with easy access to information on legalization, a particularly important source given the slow arrival of INS-sponsored publicity about the program (Hagan and Baker 1993). Publicity efforts and outreach programs by local news media, INS, and QDEs did improve with time, probably heightening program awareness. Indeed, this was especially true in Houston, where Hispanic news media tracked the program carefully. Nonetheless, for the Maya, social networks provided the detailed knowledge necessary to convert awareness into action.

It was during this period of heightened awareness and interest in legalization that many in the community began to approach me and ask about my views on legalization. One of my first observations during these visits was the absence of women in the discussions. Women were less informed about legalization than men. Their scant understanding of the process during the early months of the program can be explained partially by their position in the labor market (as domestics), which limited their interaction with other members of the Maya community. Not being well integrated into community social networks translated into limited access to information about legalization. Although the women's knowledge and interest did increase with time, their participation levels remained much lower than those of men, a finding I will discuss below (see Table 5).

By the late fall of 1987, eligibility was no longer a decisive consideration for those applying for legalization. I am not suggesting that eligibility played no role in the legalization process; rather, it took on a different meaning as perceptions of IRCA changed within the community. Initially, the issue of eligibility was taken very seriously. With time, its importance was reduced to that of a short-term technical consideration, one that could be overcome (at least for some groups in the community). Immigrants' decisions to apply became increasingly based on others' experiences and on what seemed to be relaxed restrictions by INS (Hagan and Baker 1993).

Added to the initiative taken by César and Andrés, the

experiences of two other men in the Maya community, Edgar and Miguel, triggered a rush to apply. In early April of 1988, Edgar and Miguel were picked up by INS and placed in a detention center. Both were using a company car at the time and were arrested by INS border patrol officers in Houston (which had become a border control area during the implementation of IRCA). After vigorous fund-raising within the community, the two were eventually released on fifteen hundred dollars bail. This unprecedented event had a catalytic effect on the community, for it alerted members to the very real consequences of *not* applying for legalization. The experiences of these four men largely explain the community surge in applications during the final months of the program. Over 50 percent of the applicants in the community filed during the final quarter of the program (March–May 1988). Indeed, the local INS legalization office took in over 40 percent of its total 113,870 applications during the final quarter.

Revisions in the program by INS also influenced the community's response to IRCA. The INS and immigration researchers (Meissner and Papademetriou 1988) both expected a late surge in applications, given the newness of the program and the reluctance of the undocumented population to approach INS. However, INS was not prepared for the dramatic upswing during the final weeks of the program (Baker 1990; Hagan and Baker 1993). Backlogged with mounting files at the regional level, local adjudicators in Houston were forced to renew repeatedly the temporary work-authorization cards granted to immigrants awaiting word on their cases. In April 1988, in an effort to recoup start-up costs with fee dollars and to streamline the application process, INS began to accept what they called a "skeletal application." This application consisted of little more than an application form and a check for the filing fee. Yet, upon handing in the skeletal application, the applicant received immediate work authorization and an appointment to bring in supporting documentation. These changes by INS reaffirmed many community members' rationale for applying—to buy more time to stay and work in the United States. Early in the program, community members received a decision within three months; later applicants had their work authorization cards for almost a year before their cases were adjudicated.

By the last few weeks of the filing period, the accumulated information circulating through social networks, the arrest of two fellow Maya, and the relaxed restrictions by INS had altered community perceptions about the program and impressed upon migrants the short-term advantages of seeking legal status. Increasingly, immigrants began to define the program in terms of their own immediate interests, paying little heed to the long-term implications of permanent residence or citizenship. Thus, Maya participation in the program can be seen as an adaptive settlement strategy—one entirely consistent with the sort of undocumented settlement that had characterized the community prior to IRCA.

By the time the doors to the legalization office closed on May 3, 1988, over half of the core study sample had filed petitions, although less than 15 percent were technically eligible (see Table 5). While filing an application was considered by almost all members in the community at one time or another, there was a great deal of variation within the community as to decision making and participation. Below, I explore these variations in decision making and participation.

From repeated interviews with community members throughout the program period, I found that perceptions of legalization were very different for parents, single women, and single men. Moreover, time spent in the United States also influenced the decision-making process. Each of these three groups expressed different motivations for and expectations from applying for legalization. It is to their views and voices that we now turn.

GROUP MOTIVATIONS AND EXPECTATIONS ～ Those who were firmest in their decision to legalize and most explicit in expressing the benefits they expected to derive from applying for residency were married couples with children who had lived in Houston for several years. Moreover, it was usually the woman who was most aggressive in this regard and most willing to elaborate on the reasons underlying the decision to apply, or not apply, for legalization. One married couple, both of whom qualified for legalization and who were among the first in the community to apply, gave the following reasons when asked what motivated their decision:

> Most of our family is in Houston now. We have few living relatives in Guate. María [the oldest of their two children] was born here, and both are in school here. We also just bought a house here. Our responsibility is for our children, and we think their future is better here. . . . I mean, there are more opportunities for them here than in Guate. Both our girls will finish school here.

Another couple, initially resistant to applying for legal status but who later changed their minds, gave analogous reasons for not applying:

> We have three sons in Guatemala. All are able to attend a *colegio* [private high school] there because of the money we earn here. We want to be together as a family again. We came here only to earn money, not to stay here; only to allow them greater opportunities in Guate. Our children are anxious for us to come home.

Knowing that their children were older, two of them in their teens, I asked why they did not bring them here. Claudia, the mother, responded:

> It would be wrong to take them from their grandparents and their community.

In both these cases, parents mentioned responsibility for their children as the primarily motivating factor behind the decision to apply or not apply for legal status. In the case of the first couple, owning a home and providing an education for their children impressed upon them the advantages of attaining legal security in their new country. For the latter couple, identifying with the Maya community and being separated from their children back home were barriers to settling permanently in Houston. Interestingly, the latter couple changed their minds and applied for legal status just two weeks before the program ended. They had learned of a friend who received her temporary residency card and then returned home to see her children. (With temporary residence, an immigrant can legally leave the country for a period of one month.) The couple had not seen their children in six years, fearing the consequences of an undocumented journey home. As of this writing, they maintain that they applied for temporary residence only as a means to visit their children, and they still give the same reasons for their current decision not to apply for permanent residence.

The theme of responsibility for children was also voiced by mothers outside the Maya community. During my first six months in Houston, I worked as a volunteer at a refugee hospitality house. On Wednesday evenings the refugee center held a legal clinic to assist undocumented residents living in the area. On the dozen or so occasions that I was present, I noticed that the majority of those coming in for assistance were women, many of whom requested information and help relating to legalization and political asylum. When I asked the center's volunteer attorney about this, he responded:

> I know. That has always fascinated me, too. Most of the immigrants I assist here are women. When I ask them why their husbands do not come, they repeatedly tell me the same story—that they would never apply if it was left

> up to them. A lot of these women are saving *their* earn-
> ings for the application fee and with my help [are] orga-
> nizing the paperwork. Some of their husbands don't even
> know they are here. You know, the macho thing. My
> feeling is that women are becoming increasingly more
> aggressive about issues relating to becoming legal. This
> is also fostered through the shelter, where strong female
> leadership is present. [The refugee shelter is operated by
> a Catholic sister.] But the bottom line is that women are
> coming here and doing this for their children.

My findings suggest that the mother assumes a very aggressive role in the couple's decision to apply because of her
stronger sense of responsibility to the children. Moreover, the
couple sees the decision as a permanent settlement decision,
one related to expectations concerning their children's education. Most of the migrants in the Maya community, however, are not married. As newcomers, they are typically young,
single, and without children. For the young and single members of the community, the "roots" theme does not emerge.
Within this group, though, the motivations to apply and the
expectations from the program vary by gender.

As noted above, the majority of the single men in the
community had no intention of applying initially, because
they were not eligible. Once eligibility lost its significance,
most of these young men responded to group experiences and
relaxed restrictions. If a household member applied, others
followed suit. Similarly, if one coworker or neighbor applied,
others did the same. Very few of the men decided not to apply,
reflecting the importance and influence of social networks.
While a variety of reasons were given by the single men,
many echoed the words of Oscar:

> To tell you the truth, I don't really expect to get amnes-
> ty; but I applied because, like most of us, I have nothing
> to lose from applying but everything to lose if I don't.

You heard what happened to Edgar and Miguel [the two men picked up by INS], didn't you? Well, I don't want what happened to them to happen to me. The way I look at it is, it's like paying a "coyote" to get me here. You know that's what INS is—the biggest coyote around. I pay a hundred and eighty-five dollars [the filing fee] and then I am able to work legally for another six months or so. I need to send some money home with Moses [a courier in the community], but I am also trying to save some money. I doubt if I'll even go to the interview. After my work authorization runs out, and if I get fired, I'll probably go home. I am just buying time [an increasingly common expression used by applicants during this period] to work here longer so I'll have more dollars to invest in maybe a business of some kind when I go home.

When I asked Oscar what he would do if he received temporary residence, he laughed and then responded:

I don't expect to, but even if I did, I'd probably still return home. I don't think I will get it [temporary residence], though, because where would I get the documentation to prove I was here? Even if I did, I still think I would return home. All my family, except for my brother, is in Guate. Why would I stay here when I really want to go home? What I really want to do is start a small business in Guate, maybe even in the capital, but that takes money. Anyway, I have to go back sometime to find a wife. It gets pretty lonely here when all you do is work.

Marco was the last member of the community to file his application. He literally handed in his application and fee (the INS "skeletal" filing procedure implemented during the closing days of the program) the evening before the local legalization office closed its doors for the last time. Marco had persistently told me he had no intention of applying, and when I asked him about his sudden change in plans, he said:

> I didn't even fill out all parts of the application. I just handed it to the guy at the place [legalization office] and he took it. So long as I gave the money, he would take it. This is a temporary move. I know I won't get it, but I had to try. My mother is in the hospital, and everyone is depending on me to help with the hospital bills. I think I can earn enough in six months, or until I have the interview, to help my mother and still save some. Then I'll go back, even though I don't know if I want to. I like it here. And it looks like Juan [one of his housemates and a good friend] is going to get amnesty. I'd like to stay with him and his family here in Houston. There isn't much future for me back home. Here I have a good job.

As Oscar's and Marco's comments show, neither long-term settlement, permanent residence, nor citizenship motivated the decision to apply. Indeed, they did not believe their application would succeed. Yet, the application brought with it an immediate benefit—work authorization, effective upon filing and renewable until the final decision. As Marco's and Oscar's cases illustrate, for a majority of single men in the community, the decision to apply was motivated by short-term practical concerns of economic survival and, in some cases, followed by long-term aspirations for social mobility back home. For these individuals the decision to apply was a temporary survival strategy—buying more time to work and earn money. In some cases, the needed wages are sent home to family or saved for the construction of a home in Guatemala. In other cases, there might be enough savings to start a small business in Guatemala. Although the single man is legalizing, he is not planning—at least not yet—to stay in the United States. Without the work authorization card, many believed they would lose their jobs. In the words of one, "We are paying an undocumented tax so we can stay and work." In their eyes, a hundred eighty-five dollars was a small price to pay for six months of job security.

The decision-making process for young, unmarried women is different. It features some of the same elements of reasoning we have seen in the young men of the community, yet it also resembles the responses given by many married couples. Unlike other members of the community, single women make their decisions in relative isolation from other members of the community and must take into account short-term financial considerations and long-term social realities.

Like most single men in the community, the majority of the single women had no intention of applying for legalization. They considered the option only when they became aware of the successes of others. However, the women did not benefit from information circulating through social networks to the extent that the men did. Most women in the community are domestics, and a large portion of newcomer single women are live-in domestics. They work in homes located in neighborhoods some distance from the Maya neighborhood. Most go home to the Maya community on Saturday afternoons and return to their employer's home on Sunday evening. Saturday afternoons are dedicated to keeping house (cleaning and doing laundry) for male kin and friends with whom they live on the weekends. Sundays are devoted to the week's meal preparation and to church activities.

In essence, single women are relatively isolated from others in the community. They participate in fewer community events and so have less opportunity to interact with all members of the community. When in the community over the weekends, women cook together, do laundry together, and often attend church together, but most of the time women work alone and have little opportunity to develop relations with other women. During most of the work week, their social relationships are confined to their employers and the children of their employers, with the exception of Wednesday evenings when those of the Pentecostal faith can secure a ride to meet with other women at the community church.

Because of these limitations, the women are not as well integrated into community social networks as the men. This had important implications for their level of participation in the program, since these networks were instrumental in circulating information about the advantages of legalization and the inner workings of the process. Ultimately, by not being connected to all the community networks, women were much less likely to have the information these networks provided.

During the greater part of the filing period for legalization, the success stories circulating within the community involved cases of men plus a few isolated cases of their spouses. That is to say, single women's closest contacts, other single women, were not participating in the program. Thus, not only did women not benefit from male-centered community social networks that provide information, but it is possible that their own female networks deterred them from the decision to apply.

Consequently, single women were the last group in the community to consider the application process. Many of my discussions with these women concerning their motivations and expectations in regard to legalization occurred during the final months and weeks of the program, at my apartment as they came to discuss their application files with me.

The words of one single woman, a recent arrival to the community, are similar to other newcomer women who did not apply. Twenty-three-year-old Belinda speaks:

> I don't have the hundred and eighty-five dollars to apply, and my brothers can't help me. I only earn a hundred dollars a week. They [her brothers who live in Houston] need their savings for themselves [to cover their filing

fees]. They said they would help me get legal status once they get their residency. I have only been here a short time [less than a year], and I guess I should just be happy to have a job already. And the people I work with are very nice. [She then showed me a picture of the family for whom she works.] I can't think about amnesty right now. I never really considered staying here, like others. For many of us it is just too lonely.

Hermalinda, a twenty-nine-year-old Maya who had been in Houston for five years, was very explicit in stating her reasons for applying and her expectations from the program. The following narrative comes from a compilation of comments made by Hermalinda and reflects the sentiments of many of the more established women in the community:

I need to apply for amnesty because I need to think about my future. I can't return home for several reasons. My family depends on the hundred dollars or so that I send them every month. I would have a hard time finding work in Guate as a woman. Many of the men have skills that allow them to work as tailors, and the men can always work in the milpas, but there is very little work for women there. I know some women who find work cleaning houses there, but it is not regular and pays only a few dollars a day. Most can't pay someone else to clean for them, and the embroidery work I was taught to do by my mother is now done by men on the machine. It would be hard for me to return for more than a visit. I have changed. I have been here too long to return. I am too old for marriage if I go back, and I don't want to live with my parents and be told what to do. Being a woman in Guate is very different than being a woman here. You have much greater opportunities than we have. I know that now and I want it too.

When I asked Hermalinda how she thought her life might change with legalization, she responded:

> I won't have to worry about *la migra* [INS] every time I leave the house. Sometimes I get scared just taking Minette [her employer's child] on a walk because I am afraid they [INS] will pick me up. Then what will I do? I don't speak English, he [her employer's husband] is at work, and no one could help me. Also, maybe if I get amnesty and learn English I can get a better job.

When I asked her what she meant by a better job, she responded:

> Working as a domestic during the day only, where I can earn more money and have more freedom. Maybe, if I learn English, I could actually work in a store as a cashier or something, like some of the men. Anything would be better than living here all week. It was great when I first arrived, and I really do like her [her employer]. They have been good to me. But sometimes it bothers me to be working so much for another woman. She has so much free time and yet she sometimes makes me work weekends and some evenings. The more she does that, and she does it more with time, the less I like her. I know it's not really her I don't like, but the work and long hours I'm getting tired of. There is no future in this type of work. That is why so few Americans do it. They know. If I had papers and a car, then I could at least do what Olga does [Olga is a day domestic]. She works only four days a week, no evenings, and makes more than me. [At the time of this study, the salary range for live-in domestics was ninety to a hundred sixty-five dollars a week. Hermalinda, one of the more established women, earned a hundred forty-five dollars for a five- to six-day week. In contrast, Olga and other day domestics earned as much as thirty-five to fifty dollars a day.] More important, Olga has her freedom. I never meet

anyone here. I rarely go out, except for church on Sundays. Anyway, what happens to me when the children grow up?

For many recent newcomer women, the isolation they experience in their jobs as live-in domestics and their meager savings act as potential barriers to applying for legalization. Their knowledge of "how to apply" was scant, and their social and financial resources were limited. Nonetheless, most single women, newcomer and established alike, did consider legalization, and of these, most attempted the application process. Once the decision to apply was made, they continued to face a series of financial and social barriers, a topic we will return to below. For now, let us return to the decision-making process and attempt to understand what legalization meant to the single women in the Maya community.

Like many single women in the community, Hermalinda was quite articulate about what she expected to gain. She saw legalization as a first step toward greater freedom, in general, and independence from live-in domestic work, in particular. Most single women in the community felt that the transition to day domestic work—a job which paid more and allowed greater autonomy—was the most important short-term advantage. Others also spoke of the long-term advantages of legal status—settlement options and social mobility. Like Hermalinda, they are reluctant to return to Guatemala where wage work for women is scarce and traditional gender norms prevail. With legal status, the single woman has more control over the decision to stay or to return.

The first stage of the legalization journey has shown that, among the Maya, the process of deciding to become legal varied by gender, marital status, and time spent in the receiving area. For the established married couple, regardless of the length of their settlement period, providing opportunities for their children, especially education, emerged as a central theme in the decision to legalize and, perhaps, to settle permanently in the United States. For the single man, newcomer or established, the decision to apply for legalization was a short-term adaptive strategy to acquire work authorization. Most believed they would eventually be returning to Guatemala.

Time spent in the United States appeared to have the greatest influence on the decision-making process of the single Maya woman. For the newcomer, legalization was seen as a possible ticket out of the confines of live-in domestic work. As the period of settlement grows, however, the single women increasingly grow reluctant to return home, and the becoming legal becomes an opportunity for permanent settlement. The interpersonal conflict they experience in deciding to return home or settle in the United States goes beyond the women in the Maya community. The centrality of gender to the settlement experience has been emphasized in the study of other immigrant communities as well (Pessar 1986; Grasmuck and Pessar 1991; Hondagneu-Sotelo 1992).

Whether seen as a short-term strategy to buy more time to work in the United States or as a long-term goal leading to greater freedom and social opportunities, when forced to decide, most in the Maya community eventually attempt legalization, albeit at the last minute. During the last two months of the programs' filing period, individuals were still busy gathering documents, completing applications, and generally mulling over the option of becoming residents. Let us now turn to the technical steps involved in preparing for legalization, drawing on the social experiences of the sixty or so who attempted to file their petitions.

Stage Two: Documenting Eligibility

Deciding to apply was only the beginning, for gaining legal status under the original program requirements was no easy task. It was especially difficult for some groups in the community. Applicants were required to present three types of evidence to show that they had been residing in the United

States at least since January 1, 1982: proof of residence; proof of financial responsibility; and proof of identity. If such documentation could not be collected, the immigrant was to be denied temporary residency.

In the ideal scenario, these pieces of evidence would include verifiable documents such as telephone bills, electricity bills, rent receipts, birth certificates, drivers licenses, W-2 forms, and paycheck stubs. For most of the immigrants, let alone U.S. citizens, these forms of documentation were difficult to come by, since most of the undocumented population have been living a clandestine and transient existence since their arrival in the United States. Lack of residential and employment stability makes the gathering of consistent and regular documentation very difficult indeed. Of course, there are always the exceptions. In a few cases, immigration attorneys told me about people who showed up at their offices with "suitcases" full of every possible type of record to verify their tenure in the United States. As one immigrant said to an attorney, "I've been waiting ten years for this day."

The general pattern for most immigrants in the community during the first stage of documentation included collecting all the records that could prove residency, identity, and employment. In most cases, immigrants were unable to gather adequate records to cover the entire six year period and ultimately relied on affidavits from housemates, neighbors, employers, coworkers, and other established-resident acquaintances to prove aspects of their status that could not be shown by records alone. In sum, affidavits and intermittent verifiable pieces of evidence became the most common form of documentation used by the Maya to verify their tenure in Houston. Local INS was forced to adapt to the realities of documenting an undocumented life.

The use of affidavits as the major source of documentation was not exclusive to the Maya community. Early in the implementation of IRCA, agencies (e.g., QDEs and local INS) discovered that the legalization "ideal type"—an applicant with a well-organized stack of rent receipts, paycheck stubs, and identity documents spanning nearly six years—would rarely pass through the doors of the legalization office (Baker 1990). Initially, INS required a document for every month the applicant was in the country. Then it shifted to one document per quarter. By the final quarter of the program, affidavit-based cases came to be recognized as a necessary adaptation to the realities of undocumented life. The trend toward a more inclusionary posture in the acceptance of documentation evolved during the implementation phase: as early applications fell far below planning projections nationwide and as INS officials watched "real people flow through the application process," they came to recognize how difficult it was for an undocumented person to gather the comprehensive paperwork requested (Hagan and Baker 1993). Moreover, by relying exclusively on user fees to fund the legalization program (staff training, hiring, equipment, etc.), INS had little choice but to relax its documentary restrictions. In Houston, where INS officials felt they had been underfunded since the program's onset and where the hope was that high application rates would influence budgetary decisions, this came to be an important consideration.

Although relaxed documentation requirements certainly triggered a rush of applications in the final quarter of the program, even the collecting of affidavits proved difficult for some. This research revealed that documentation was much harder to come by in the case of those employed in the informal sector of the labor market. These are jobs where wages are arbitrary, where no employee benefits are provided, and where state regulation is not a factor. People holding these jobs had an especially difficult time verifying residency and employment. In my sample, almost all of the men were employed in the formal sector of the labor market, as maintenance workers in a large retail chain, while most of the women were employed in the informal sector as day or live-in domestics (see Table 4). Three dimensions of the work and overall settlement experience of women—the nature of their work relations, their restricted participation in community social networks, and their limited development of relationships outside the immigrant community—made it more difficult for women to gather the documentation necessary to legalize.

With the assistance of other women in the community, all female newcomers are directed into a narrow sector of the economy, usually working as a live-in domestic five or six days a week and returning to the community neighborhood on the weekend. As a live-in domestic, one's work relations are necessarily confined to the employer's family, with most of the interaction occurring between the domestic and her female employer. These women, as is the case with others working in the informal sector, are most often paid in cash. This makes it difficult for them to verify their residence and employment. Consequently, when it came time for these women to gather documentation for legalization, they found they were dependent on affidavits from only one source, the employer, who usually refused to provide them. In eighteen cases I was approached by women in the community to act as an intermediary in the collection of documentation from their employers. The reasons given by one employer, Martha (a thirty-four-year-old working professional and mother of one), for refusing to provide documentation for her domestic (a Maya woman who had been working in the house for almost three years) follows and is a common story:

> When you first called me I didn't think there would be any problem writing an affidavit stating Graciela had been working for us, since it would only be stating the facts and it would help Graciela. However, I spoke with my husband about it because, to be perfectly honest, I

really don't know much about the law. He said definitely not. I also talked to my mother and several close friends who have domestics and they also advised against it.

When I alerted her to the fact that she would be protected under the grandfather clause of IRCA, which does not penalize those employers who hired persons prior to the law's inception (November 6, 1986), she responded:

Now you know I would really like to help Graciela. She is a great worker, an honest woman, and my daughter just adores her. They have become quite attached. But we both are a bit nervous about the legal implications of writing such an affidavit. It's not sanctions we are worried about. You see we haven't paid any social security for Graciela in the past, and now we would have to report all that and, well, with my husband being a lawyer it would make things a bit sticky. He won't bend on this. He is convinced that INS might report us to IRS. I am sorry but we just can't take the risk.

Most of the live-in domestics in the community reversed their decision to legalize when they learned that their employers were unwilling to provide documentation, but some did not give up. Graciela, for example, quit working for Martha shortly after the above incident and found work with a new employer who was willing to sponsor her throughout the legalization program, an exceptional situation. Shortly after Graciela left, Martha called and asked if I could locate another domestic to take Graciela's place. Like many of the employers I spoke with, Martha appeared more concerned about the financial implications of having broken the law (i.e., not paying social security) in the past than about the implications of employer sanctions, which impose fines on employers who hired undocumented workers after November 6, 1986.

Martha's actions were not surprising, given that during

this period employer sanctions were not an operating priority among local INS enforcement agencies. Nor was the arrest of undocumented domestics a high priority for INS nationwide. The rationale for not searching private residences centers around the fact that domestic work is not a lucrative position coveted by U.S. citizens. At the time of the study, there had only been one such arrest in Texas (Houston Chronicle 1988). In retrospect, Martha's concerns proved prescient. The experiences of Zoe Baird and several other potential Clinton appointees, which became known as Nannygate, reflected precisely the issues that worried Martha and her husband along with most other employers of the domestics in the study sample.

Unable to secure help from their employers, women were forced to turn to those members of the immigrant community whom they knew. Unfortunately, while these networks were helpful in assisting the newcomer in finding a job upon arrival in Houston, they acted as a hindrance in the documentation process. These restrictive networks could not provide useful information to the seeker of the documentation. Moreover, as some domestics in the network, unable to find documentation, reverse their decision to apply, this influences the decision of other women who might apply. Thus, only one of the live-in domestics in the sample reported to me that she had found documentation using the help of other domestics in the community. Unable to obtain documentation from her own employer, Stella managed to secure work verification through a friend's employer, who, in an unusual act, assisted three women (two Maya and one Mexican) by providing affidavits stating she had hired all three to do day work in the past.

Women were also disadvantaged in the legalization process because they did not have ties to acquaintances and networks outside the community, the primary supplier of residential verification. The lack of ties outside the community was evident in many cases. For example, women were much more likely than men to approach me and ask me to write an affidavit stating I knew them. One single woman, Sonya, upon learning that her employer refused to supply documentation, was so desperate that she literally went door-to-door in the employer's neighborhood looking for a familiar face who might be willing to assist her.

Of the nine women who managed to secure the necessary documentation to apply for amnesty, four worked as day domestics and seven were married. All of the day domestics were able to locate an employer who would provide an affidavit verifying employment. In most cases, day domestics worked for several employers at one time. Consequently, the chances of finding one willing employer were greater, especially because the potential financial implications for the employer of a day domestic are less onerous. Additionally, because they live in the community neighborhood and not at the employer's residence, day domestics found it easier to verify residency. It was also less difficult for married than for single domestics to locate documentation, because the former could recruit assistance from the husband's network.

It was less difficult for men to verify their employment and residency in the Houston area. For one thing, since the majority of the men were working in a regulated industry, employers were more willing to provide documentation and coworkers were more willing to provide affidavits. Also, as men were more integrated into community social networks, they had wider access to information about others' experiences than the women. In sum, men had developed social ties with established residents in the host society—coworkers, fellow parishioners in the Catholic church, members of other soccer teams, and neighbors. All of these outside ties are utilized during the documentation process.

Most research on immigrant settlement emphasizes the advantages of social networks for the newcomer migrant, not how these same personal networks, based on family, kin, and friends, might impede some aspect of settlement over time.

We have seen how the Maya community draws on these networks during the initial stages of settlement to find housing and jobs, and we have seen the role of networks in circulating information about how to legalize. However, these migrant-based social networks also have their disadvantages, especially as the period of settlement increases. Locked into a given network, the immigrants have available only the resources of that one group. Thus, while these social networks may help newcomers find jobs, they are also likely to restrict their job mobility, since the migrants do not develop outside resources to use in changing jobs. Unless migrants are able to establish ties with others outside the original social network (e.g., other immigrants and established residents in the receiving area), their settlement opportunities, over time, may become restricted. Migrants can, in fact, become so encapsulated within these networks that they lose some of the advantages found in developing relationships outside the community. This was certainly the case with the Maya women whose jobs made it very difficult for them to develop the outside relationships needed to facilitate documentation and, ultimately, legalization.

Granovetter's (1973) distinction between "strong ties" and "weak ties" is useful to demonstrate the limits of personal-based networks in the settlement of the Maya community, especially as they influenced legalization opportunities. Briefly, Granovetter showed that weak ties (those between acquaintances) can provide more social mobility opportunities than strong ties (those between family and close friends) because the former bridges two groups, thereby maximizing flows of information and increasing resources.

Remember, that although the women and men of the Maya community were equally confined to strong personal ties during the initial settlement stage, over time, men had the advantage in the legalization process: they were able to develop relationships with established residents at work, through the soccer league, and in their neighborhoods. These

weak ties proved invaluable when it came to securing affidavits to document residency. In contrast, women, because of
their labor-market conditions, were unable to develop relationships with established residents. Confined to these personal networks, and the strong ties on which they are based,
their pool of resources was limited. The process of securing
affidavits for their application files became arduous, if not
impossible. Thus, although most of the women made the
decision to legalize, many were unable to pass through the
second stage of the legalization journey—collecting documentation.

For most in the community, then, documenting tenure in
the United States began as a difficult process. Unable to
secure the most desirable forms of documentation (W-2 forms,
rent receipts, electricity bills), most were forced to rely almost exclusively on affidavits supplied by employers, coworkers and established-resident neighbors. Once INS relaxed its
documentation requirements, collecting documentation was
transformed into a relatively painless process. As Table 5
shows, many of the Maya applicants in the study sample were
technically ineligible, having arrived after the January 1982
cutoff date. Nonetheless, more than half the study sample
applied successfully and were granted temporary resident
status. The exception to this pattern was among the women
in the community. Their low participation can be explained
by their more restrictive networks as compared to those of the
men.

Stage Three: Adjudicating for Temporary Residency

Once an immigrant had compiled his or her documentation,
he or she reviewed it to ensure it was in order and then
submitted the application to an official at the local INS office.
As mentioned earlier, since most undocumented have been
accustomed to viewing INS as an adversary, Congress stipulated

that voluntary agencies and community organizations (QDEs) be allowed to prescreen legalization applicants in order to encourage participation. The INS originally estimated that up to 80 percent of applicants would opt for this method; however, only 21 percent of all applicants, both nationwide and in Houston, went through QDEs (Baker 1990). According to national figures, only about 8 percent of all legalization applicants were aided by lawyers, while most chose to apply directly with INS. At the local and national level, INS took considerable pains to pat itself on the back for directly recruiting so many to the legalization offices.

While the INS was quick to interpret this direct contact with the immigrants as a public relations victory—overcoming the "fear factor" touted in Congress—we found that QDEs were crucial in disseminating clear information to the local immigrant community via Spanish-language media. Moreover, as discussed and elaborated on above, their reinterpretation of their legalization role from administrative to activist certainly led to the liberalization of eligibility standards (Hagan and Baker 1993).

The story of the Maya's adjudication experience reveals a more complicated picture of the application process—one that emphasizes the temporal dimension of applying and the role of another key, but silent, actor in the application process.

During the first few months of the program, the community remained wary and distrustful of INS, and immigrants were not likely to go directly to a legalization office to file. The logical recourse, according to observers of the law, would be to seek assistance from a QDE. Immigrants filing from the Maya community, however, did not have close ties with many of the service organizations acting as QDEs. In fact, none of the community immigrants who applied reported seeking out assistance from a QDE. Some early applicants (13 percent) chose Hispanic lawyers, people they "could communicate [with] and depend on." The cost of hiring a lawyer varied from five hundred to a thousand dollars, depending on the difficulty of the case and the particular lawyer. According to several in the community, this method was most desirable because "the lawyer goes with you to the office and represents you at the interview." Most, however, including the majority of Maya applicants, could not afford this method.

Most migrants in the community filed during the last months of the application period and sought assistance from neighborhood, Spanish-speaking notarios with whom they were more culturally familiar. As noted above, notaries benefited from the fact that the notary public serves as the functional equivalent to legal counsel in much of Latin America, including Guatemala. Notaries were willing to compile, organize, and notarize papers for about a hundred and fifty dollars. In most cases, names of notaries were obtained from others who had used their services. Thus, a legalization network developed among applicants in the community. They shared information about access to services and about their experiences with different attorneys, notaries, and INS officials. In the final analysis, four or five notaries did the bulk of the paperwork for the entire community. The only exception to this pattern was a select group of immigrants who had established contacts with U.S. residents (employers, close friends) who were willing to assist them.

Those in the community who filed late in the application period employed notaries to review their documents and then went in person to submit their own applications at the local legalization office. When I asked how they felt about the upcoming meeting with INS, most responded in a fashion similar to José's.

> Well, at first I was scared. I mean, four months I have been thinking about this, and if I could have gotten a lawyer I would have. With a lawyer you are sure. But then, everyone is doing it [submitting their own applications], and la migra isn't deporting them when they hand

in their application. They don't make the final decision, just recommendations. They just want our money.

Graciela echoed José's decreasing fear:

I'm not as nervous as I was a few months ago. I know so many people who have done it and had no problem. They have people who speak Spanish. So long as I have the money, that's all they are really concerned with. So, I am not as scared as I once was, but my *patrona* [her employer] is coming with me, just in case.

Yet another, a twenty-one-year-old single man, expressed minimum anxiety. In fact, his comments indicated he was fully aware of what to expect upon arrival at the legalization office, even knowing which adjudicators were most lenient in the reviewing process:

No, I am not worried. I haven't heard of any really bad experiences, at least within the community. I have been told that I will probably have to wait all day before I see someone, even though my appointment is for eight in the morning. They make everyone's appointment for eight. Once you're in the office you can't leave, so everyone brings food with them. I was also told that the clerks get upset if the file is not completely in order. The notary said they care more about how the file is presented than about what is in it. Juan and José told me to try to get an interview with Mrs. Rodríguez because she is more understanding than the other clerks and is more likely to give you a good recommendation.

A young immigrant couple had good things to say about how they were treated treatment at the INS legalization office:

Actually, they were very nice to us. The hardest part was waiting, because it took all day and we had our baby with us. Once we saw the clerk, it [the interview] took only about fifteen minutes. And the woman who reviewed our papers spent more time with our baby than she did looking over our papers. And she told us right then that she was giving us a good recommendation. Everyone tells us we were lucky to get a woman. We feel we were very lucky to have her, as she decided our future.

Most members of the community began to see the agency as a money-making operation, not just an enforcement arm of the law. Most related positive experiences about the time spent at the legalization office. Part of this had to do with others' positive experiences, and part had to do with the fact that all received work authorization cards upon completion of the interview. Moreover, fear of INS, especially its enforcement features, had decreased dramatically by the time most were ready to submit their applications. At the local level, INS officials spent considerable time reaching out to their target population, both before and during the legalization filing period. As mentioned, INS officials were guests on Spanish-speaking radio and television stations, and they organized and attended neighborhood community meetings to improve their relationship with Houston's Hispanic community and to encourage participation in the program. No longer viewing INS solely as an enforcement arm of the law, many began to see the agency as a business and responded by going directly to the INS via a notary whose exclusive task was organization of the file. Their experiences in the interview bore out their changing attitude toward INS.

TWO PRINCIPAL PATTERNS emerge from the social process of legalization we have just examined. First, the strong internal community structure facilitated participation in the legalization program. Maya social networks provided resources to draw upon during legalization—the most important being information about how the system worked. Moreover, since men's networks included relationships with established residents, they were able to draw on these new resources and act on their decision to legalize. For the women, however, the documentation requirements were especially hard because of the nature of their work and their more restricted and less resourceful networks, which made it impossible to obtain records without the assistance of their employer or their male partners. Secondly, because the legalization program offered immediate benefits that responded to Maya needs, turnout was enhanced. By providing immediate work authorization, the INS played into the settlement strategies of the Maya, eligible or not, who sought to keep as many options open for as long as possible.

In the following chapter, we shall look at some emergent changes in the immigrant community—changes that are a result of strong community participation in the legalization program.

CHAPTER FIVE

LIFE AFTER LEGALIZATION

WE CANNOT KNOW THE LONG-TERM SOCIAL EFFECTS of the legalization program for some time. As history has so often demonstrated, it takes years—even generations—to recognize the unanticipated social effects of immigration policies. The passage of IRCA is no exception. It will take a lifetime for the effects of this policy to manifest themselves.

Our inability to forecast the social and demographic ramifications of IRCA, especially its impact on immigrant communities, is partly a result of our lack of sufficient knowledge about how immigrants actively respond to state intervention—about the strategies they employ to overcome perceived or real obstacles to state policies that attempt to regulate their settlement behavior. By treating the Maya as active agents of the settlement process, rather than as passive targets of policy reform, I have taken the first step toward tackling the problem of how to assess or predict the impact of IRCA on immigrant communities. In doing so, I have thus far shown how immigrant communities interpret policy and actually produce outcomes not envisioned by policymakers.

Eligible or not, many in the Maya community successfully made their way through the legalization process.

A further complication in assessing the effects of legalization on changes in the immigrant community—one that will become readily apparent to the reader as the present chapter progresses—is the difficult task of determining the extent to which these changes can be explained specifically by the legalization process, as opposed to long-term settlement in the United States. Despite this confounding factor, what I attempt to show in the following discussion is that the effects of legalization are tangible, in that legal status enables previously undocumented persons to take advantage, either directly or indirectly, of opportunities previously reserved for U.S. residents and citizens.

In this final chapter of the story of legalization, then, I examine some of the emergent community changes engendered by legalization. Let me stress the emergent character of these patterns and the cautionary tone of the ensuing discussion, for community changes associated with legalization are in process. Equally important, I am no longer living within the community to observe such changes.

Years have passed since I reluctantly ended my three years in the field and removed myself from the lives and the homes of the Totonicapán Maya in Houston. Since my departure from the community in 1990, however, I have continued to follow the settlement experiences of roughly a dozen members of the original study sample. Their thoughts and observations concerning community change, along with my own and those of my fellow researcher, Nestor Rodríguez, are incorporated into the following discussion. In addition, in the summer of 1990, I was fortunate to travel to the home community with a newly legalized cohort of Maya. They were returning home to San Pedro, some for the first time in many years, to visit family and friends and share in two community celebrations: the Fiesta de Santiago (an annual celebration of the

town's patron saint) and the quinceañera of one of the younger sisters of a Houston Maya woman, who had asked me to
accept the honored role of *padrina* (Godmother). Conversa-   *madrina*
tions with return migrants and discussions with family members who have sons, daughters, brothers, and sisters in Houston
are also incorporated into my observations in San Pedro.

When I moved out of the community in the spring of
1990, the initial ramifications of IRCA for the community
were just emerging. At the time of my departure, forty-one
Maya—or just over half of the study sample—had successfully transformed their immigration status from undocumented
to temporary resident, and most were in the process of meeting the technical qualifications for permanent resident status.[1]
Most agreed that two factors led to the decision to apply for
permanent residence: 1. the ability to travel legally between
Houston and Guatemala and, 2. the opportunity to petition for
spouses and children to join them in the United States.[2]

Being granted temporary or permanent resident status is
not just an adjustment in legal status; it also represents
important changes in all the social and psychological dimensions associated with being undocumented. Once the fear of
being undocumented is lifted from the shoulders of the immigrant, he or she begins to demonstrate new levels of confidence and assertiveness that translate into greater control
over one's life. In a sense, the transition from undocumented
to resident frees the immigrant from a life in which actions
are always risky and tentative at best. With legal status,
immigrants are more inclined to think of their actions as
permanent commitments and to perceive choices as opportunities rather than risks. At the individual, group, and community level, new patterns of behavior begin to evol
more of the Maya make the transition from undocu
status to temporary or permanent residency. With
frequency, these emerging patterns include 1. legi
identity in the United States; 2. evolving relati

newly legalized members of the community and established U.S. residents; 3. shifting power relations between men and women in the Houston community; 4. housing and residential changes in Houston; 5. aspirations to social mobility; and 6. increased interaction between Houston and Guatemala, resulting in further migration—both legal and undocumented—to Houston.

👥 LEGITIMATION OF IDENTITY IN THE HOST COMMUNITY

After the arrival of their temporary residence cards, the newly legalized Maya began to initiate steps toward legitimizing their identity in the United States. Falsified social security cards were discarded and replaced with legitimate ones. Hidden dollars are placed in newly opened checking and savings accounts. Insurance was obtained for uninsured automobiles and, for the first time, the new residents filed their income tax forms.

Initially, new residents approached me to assist with these matters, as they were hesitant about dealing with U.S. bureaucracies. For example, at their request, I accompanied three single women on their first visit to a bank to open up savings accounts. My role was that of cultural broker, introducing them to the bank protocol and translating their requests to the bank representative. In their case, as with many, fear of being unable to communicate because of the language barrier was the primary reason for avoiding interaction with bureaucracies. This fear, however, gradually lessened as the new residents learned of the widespread use of Spanish in communication between Houston's residents and bureaucracies. The transition from a resident in need of assistance to a self-reliant member of society is best illustrated by the case of Antonio, a twenty-three-year-old Maya who had received his temporary residence card one month prior to the following event.

Antonio dropped by to see if I could call IRS for him. Like many of the male immigrants in the community, he had falsely claimed to be married in order to reduce the amount of taxes withheld from his monthly paychecks. Having legal residency, he told me, impressed upon him the need to legitimate other aspects of his life. "I have to do things right now. Otherwise they may take away my second card. [His first card was a work authorization card.] They know where I live and work. It's not the same anymore."

Antonio learned of another new resident who was paying his back taxes on a monthly basis. Not being able to pay in one shot the, roughly, thousand dollars he owed, Antonio asked if I would call and inquire about a payment plan. The call was answered by a woman who, upon learning that I was calling for a non-English-speaking new resident, told me that a Spanish-speaking clerk was available to assist Antonio. Thus, Antonio was able to resolve the situation without my further assistance. I have since learned that he recently obtained car insurance and opened a savings account. Access to Spanish-speaking personnel makes a difference.

Carlos, a Salvadoran who lived in the Maya neighborhood and was a friend to many in the community, dramatically shifted his identity as a consequence of legalization. Upon receiving his "green card," Carlos joined the U.S. Army and is currently stationed in Germany. Joining the army would not have been possible without legal status. His decision to do so reflects a major commitment to the military establishment and U.S. society; more important, it provides a range of new and unprecedented opportunities. As Carlos told me in a recent phone call from Germany, "I would never have joined the army back home. I know there is no future in such a job there. But here it is different. I can see the world. And once I am out, they will pay for my education."

The three young women, Antonio, and Carlos all see themselves as residents and participants in a new society. All are taking advantage of opportunities available through their newly acquired status. To do so, they must also legitimate themselves through interactions with U.S. institutions and bureaucracies. What is relevant here is that participating in legalization appears to accelerate the process of acquiring the emblems of North American identity—whether opening a bank account, obtaining car insurance, paying taxes, learning the English language and U.S. history or, in the exceptional case, joining the army. Moreover, this process is generally learned only by the newly legalized members community.

Some of the new residents are even adopting aspects of Texas culture, most evidenced in changes in consumption patterns. Once satisfied with a cash purchase of a used Nissan or Toyota pickup, temporary residents are now financing brand-new Broncos and family cars. This is an interesting development, and it appears to be part related to changes both in legalization and in settlement plans. Many of the immigrants originally bought Toyotas and Nissans because these cars are common in Guatemala. As one immigrant explained, when I asked him why everyone drives Nissans or Toyota pickups:

> No, I didn't own a car in Guate. Most of us, except Santos [a courier], didn't either. However, in Guate people who do own cars usually drive Nissans and Toyotas; in the countryside, they use Nissan and Toyota pickups. That's because those are the only cars for which we can get parts and service. They make those parts in Guate. So people here buy them so that when they return, they can take them with them.

Switching car types and upgrading one's car demonstrates, I believe, a shift to adopting the commercial aspects of Texan culture in the anticipation that the United States will become one's home. More important, in making such a purchase the immigrant is aware that he will probably be around for the several years it takes to pay off the car. While I have observed several other changes in life-style and consumption patterns (e.g., modernization of women's hairstyles and clothing), those changes do not appear to be directly linked to legalization; rather, they seem related to settlement stages and the amount of time spent in the United States.

♟ EVOLVING INTERGROUP RELATIONS

Another interesting development is the effect the legalization program has had on newcomer–established resident relations. Basically, my findings suggest that relations between newcomer applicants for legalization and established U.S. residents have been created, transformed, and often strengthened as a result of initial contact during the process of documentation. Recall, almost all legalization applicants approached coworkers, employers, neighbors, and fellow parishioners for affidavits. Over time, relations that were initially based on assistance have become more congenial and have extended into a variety of social activities.

This pattern is illustrated by several migrants in my sample who applied for legalization. For example, two Maya newcomers, Jaime and Manuel, sought documentation assistance from Anglo residents. Jaime relied primarily on Anglo coworkers and neighboring tenants, while Manuel requested assistance from Anglo members of his church. As a result of seeking documentation from established residents, Jaime and Manuel are now participating in various social activities (e.g., playing pool and watching football, not soccer, games) with the Anglos who helped them. At a birthday party for Jaime's child, several Anglo coworkers and neighbors mingled with Maya newcomers. To accommodate the English-speaking guests, the traditional "Happy Birthday" song was sung in both Spanish and English, and rock-and-roll followed the marimba music that is traditional at such community events.

Legal status also translates into greater assertiveness on the part of immigrant groups, who then reach out and form relationships of mutual benefit with established-resident groups. Recall that, initially, the Totonicapán Maya had formed two soccer teams but that, over time, decreasing participation and support from community members led to only one team remaining. Things changed, however, with the acquisition of legal status by key team members. Rather than trying to rely solely on dwindling community support, the Maya team reached out to a neighborhood community organization for assistance with the formation of a soccer league. The organization acted as an administrative broker, finding playing fields for the teams. The Maya team captain at this time was Juan, the pioneer of the community, who convinced other immigrant teams (Peruvians, Salvadorans, and others) to join the league. Again, without legal status, Juan said he would have been less likely to approach other teams or the neighborhood organization for assistance. In Juan's view, being a resident "gave him the right" to use the public parks. In the final analysis, it was a cooperative venture of established organizations and the newly legalized Maya cohort that led to the development of the currently active soccer league.

On another occasion, a group of newly legalized Maya who were planning a visit to Guatemala, reached out to established residents involved in health care and social work to help collect medical supplies for a clinic in Totonicapán. The established-resident group, who call themselves Amigos de San Pedro (Friends of San Pedro), became so involved in the effort that they accompanied the Maya to Totonicapán to deliver the supplies. A description of their visit, along with its implications for creating organizational links between the two communities, will be elaborated on below, in a section on interaction between Houston and Totonicapán.

♟ CHANGING GENDER RELATIONS

Relations between groups within the community may also have been transformed by legalization. In Chapter Three, I argued that Maya women face a seemingly contradictory settlement experience. On the one hand, because parents are not around and because the women rely on weekend housing in men's homes (women live at the employer's house during the week), they are increasingly dependent on men in the community. On the other hand, being employed and earning income for the first time translates into greater financial and social autonomy for many of these women.

My findings in regard to changes in these relationships as a result of legalization are tentative, but nonetheless, warrant attention. Recall that most who received legal status were men. In interviews with at least six undocumented women who are romantically involved with legalized men, I learned that legal status has been converted into an emerging source of power imbalance between the sexes. For example, one young Maya woman, recently separated from her husband, is now considering moving back into his household since he promised he would petition for a visa for her once he received permanent residency. Another young man in the community threatened on several occasions to withhold the future promise of securing legal status for his live-in partner. Yet another young woman refuses to leave her live-in partner, even though he beats her, because "I need legal status for my children's future." This pattern has been echoed by community workers and immigration attorneys who serve the undocumented. Attorneys and social workers who work with undocumented women have observed an increase in domestic assaults on women, an increase linked to their unclear status vis-à-vis the legalized partner or husband (Fuentes 1988).

Other studies have pointed to the greater control exerted by men over women in the migration process (Simon and Bretell 1986). My findings indicate that legalization may exacerbate this control, because the woman becomes increasingly dependent upon the newly legalized man to petition for her legal resident status. Moreover, if the woman has left the man, the burden may be even greater, since the man controls the papers. This is especially relevant, given that the Maya community includes many remaining undocumented single women as well as many undocumented newcomers who hope their husbands, partners, and immediate family will petition for their permanent resident status.

Even those women who are married are caught in a Catch-22 situation. Although wives (and minor children) of legalized aliens are protected from deportation and some are permitted to work, they do not enjoy the same benefits as husbands who are legalized (e.g., freedom to travel out of the country).[3] Wives are increasingly dependent on their husbands to petition for their visas. Moreover, through follow-up conversations with primary informants in the community, I learned that only five wives in the whole community have obtained such visas. Ultimately, legal status may become a resource to be withheld or released, depending on the whim of the man and the existing state of the relationship.

♀♂ HOUSING AND RESIDENTIAL CHANGES

The acquisition of legal status has also enabled some Maya in Houston to enter a fourth stage of settlement—home ownership (see Chapter Three for a description of stages one through three). Several more-established families in the community sold their small farms in Guatemala, took advantage of the city's collapsed real-estate market and declining interest rates, and put down payments on new homes, which are located miles away from the Maya community. One could raise the point that homeownership is a function of long-term residency and Houston's low-cost housing; however, it is also directly related to legal status. Prospective homeowners must present proof of legal status to financial institutions in order to qualify for a loan.

The pioneers in the community, Juan and Carmen, expressed the following reasons for buying a home and moving away from the Maya neighborhood:

> We moved because, once we got our green card [permanent residence], we realized I could start to make plans for my family. The schools are better where we live now. They even have ESL [English as a second language] classes for my children. Why should I keep paying rent if I can buy a house? Having Pablo and Edgar [Juan's brothers-in-law] living with us helps with the mortgage. It's the right thing to do if you have a family.

Home ownership is a move taken only by families who have accumulated a certain amount of capital and who see their residence in the United States as permanent. Juan and Carmen, for example, are also among the few Maya who have tentatively decided to seek naturalization in the future.

Still other new residents move away from the community to areas in the city where rental prices are even lower than those found in the Maya neighborhood. These new residents emphasize the long-term advantages of residential change for their children but also remark on the short-term disadvantages of being away from the community. These sentiments are expressed most often by mothers. Patty, a twenty-two-year-old woman, lives with her husband, their U.S.-born son, a fellow Maya from San Pedro and, until recently, another friend, also from San Pedro. The following reflections were expressed by Patty some months after she left the community:

> Yes, it's very nice out here. For the same rent we get a washing machine, and Jorge [her son] has lots of children to play with. But I get lonely. Juan [her husband] works all the time [six days a week, as a baker] and I only get out once a week to work, when Juan or Marco is home to take care of Jorge. I talk to Ana [a friend in the community] every day on the phone. But it's not the same. You know, that's why Marco [the young man who filed his skeletal application the evening before the legalization office closed. He had lived with Patty and Juan since his arrival in Houston] moved back to the apartment complex [one of three in the Maya neighborhood]; he was lonely. As much as he loves Jorge, he missed the community more. I still think Juan made the right decision, [to move away from the community] but it's hard for me. He doesn't understand. It's going to be really difficult for me when he goes home to visit and takes Jorge with him. [Like many women who did not apply for legal status, she will be forced to stay in the United States while her husband makes the trip to San Pedro to visit family and friends.]

Residential changes in the community will continue. Since the late 1980s the Houston economy has been picking up, and rental property in the Maya neighborhood is on the rise. Many of the Maya have been forced to move into cheaper rental property, located even farther away from their jobs, in the far western sector of the city. The apartment complex where I lived for three years among the Maya has been completely renovated, and rental prices have almost doubled (from $200 to $375 a month for one bedroom), forcing most of the Maya farther west into several different apartment complexes. As a result of residential changes in the community, the households are more dispersed and opportunities for daily interaction across households have been somewhat hampered, while the opportunities for interaction with established residents in more multiethnic neighborhoods have increased.

♔ ASPIRATIONS TO SOCIAL MOBILITY

One of the questions that continues to dominate the post-IRCA research agenda is whether legal status affects social mobility (Tienda and Singer, forthcoming; Borjas and Tienda, 1994; Donato and Massey 1993; Bailey 1985; Massey 1987b). Simply put, the key question is: Have immigrants gotten better jobs as a result of legal status? Among the Totonicapán Maya, the answer is basically no. To date, none of the Maya in the study sample who received legal status has experienced significant occupational mobility or earned higher wages in the U.S. labor market. Some of the men of the larger Totonicapán community who have legalized have left the supermarket chain for which they initially worked and are working for either a local movie theater chain or a restaurant chain. Of these, a few chose to leave, two were fired, and several lost their jobs while on extended visits to Guatemala. The jobs they hold, however, are in low-skilled maintenance positions (e.g., janitors, dishwashers) and, so, do not reflect occupational mobility. Their entry into these firms, however, could lead to the development of more diverse male-based job networks in the Maya community.

A handful of the men in the core study sample have changed jobs since acquiring legal status, but not for better ones in the U.S. labor market. Interestingly, these include five or so entrepreneurs who left their jobs in the supermarket chain and entered the informal economy as couriers between the Houston and Guatemalan communities. This change is a direct result of legalization, as their new legal status allows them to travel freely across international borders. Once dominated by only a few Maya who had visas, now the courier service has become much more competitive, including close to a dozen active couriers of both sexes.

Julio, one of the long-term residents in the Maya community (Juan's brother-in-law) and a key informant in this study, had been promoted to the position of bagger in the supermarket chain and was earning upwards of nine dollars an hour, including tips, just before he went into the courier business. He is now living in the town center of San Pedro (he grew up in one of the neighboring communities), in the home he built with money made in Houston. I visited with Julio recently, while he was in Houston purchasing a truck to sell in Guatemala and collecting goods from the community in Houston to bring to households in San Pedro. I told him I was surprised by his decision to leave the supermarket, given he had just been promoted and would probably continue to move up the firm's employment ladder. Julio was one of the very few members of the community to have completed high school in Guatemala. He has a strong command of English, having studied it a bit in Guatemala and in Houston. I always assumed he would settle in the United States permanently, despite his repeated claims of wanting to return home one day. During our visit he discussed his reasons for becoming a courier and moving back to Guatemala. Chief among them were the desire to find a "more traditional" Maya wife (meaning one who had not lived in Houston) and to become a teacher in Guatemala. Until he could do this he could work as a courier and enjoy both cultures. Clearly, Julio's aspirations are for social mobility in Guatemala. He recognizes that his chances of becoming a teacher in the United States are limited, and he earns a nice living as a courier. Interestingly, his girlfriend and, perhaps, future wife, wants to move to

Houston. Most in the community are betting on his moving back here.

Should we be surprised that the majority of the legalized men in the Maya community have not moved on to better jobs or experienced significant improvements in their wages? Julio is an exception. Upon arrival in Houston, all assumed unskilled positions in the secondary labor market and most do not have the basic skills (e.g., verbal or written command of English) to improve their position in the labor market. The acquisition of these skills takes time and desire.

As I've mentioned in several places in this book, most of the men in the community are employed by a single, but fast-growing retail supermarket chain and make up the bulk of the maintenance and produce staff. A few of the workers have been promoted, but these promotions were due to a new director's policy and to the length of time in the company, rather than any new legal status. Except for those men in the community who entered the courier business, none of the remaining legalized men in the study sample with whom I have spoken since I moved out of the community has voiced a desire to leave the company. They feel a high degree of loyalty to the company because it has provided economic security since their arrival. They have fared well, very well in some cases. At this time, it is hard to envision another employment opportunity that would allow the immigrant workers so much control over the labor process. Recall, for example, that the work-related networks operate under the supervision of a fellow Maya (the encargado, as he is referred to by his fellow Maya at work), who allows them to negotiate schedules with other immigrants in the crew. This enables an immigrant to travel home to Guatemala for a visit without fear of losing his job. Given that the directors of some of the stores in the company now require documentation, we can expect that it will be harder for newcomers to enter the company. For most of the Maya men in the community, however, the influence of legal status on employment, wages, and promotions within the company is dependent on the use of the immigrant job networks and on time at the job.

The mobility question is a bit more complicated with respect to the women in the community, largely because they are less satisfied with their jobs and are therefore more anxious to improve their labor market status. The domestic workers, while being most vocal about aspirations to job mobility, are reluctant to leave domestic work. The half-dozen or so live-in domestics who have acquired legal status, either through the legalization program or through "family fairness," speak of planning to become day domestics and hope eventually to move into retail work. In their view, either move would provide far more autonomy than they have as live-in domestics. But they are aware that mobility does not occur only as a result of changes in legal status. As one young woman told me, "Now that I have legal status, there is a possibility of getting a better job. That is why I applied. I'd like to work in a store, somewhere where I can meet other people. But first I have to learn English and save enough for a car."

Knowledge of English and access to good transportation are additional prerequisites to leaving domestic work. Several of the women are attending English classes at schools in their neighborhoods and are saving for a car.

There is another issue in the mobility equation. During my last visits with the domestics in the study sample, most were waiting for their green cards. The women repeatedly voiced a reluctance to change jobs while they are in the process of altering their legal status. Adjusting one's legal status involves a series of changes in one's life—ranging from trips back to Guatemala, to regularizing one's identity in the United States, to enrolling in English classes. All these changes take time and money; so it is logical to seek stability in at least one dimension of life (viz., work and residency). In fact, if legal status has any effect on social mobility, in the short-run, at least, it appears to be through its indirect effect on job security. Having employment security frees the immigrant to take advantage of other opportunities (e.g., English classes, continuation of school) that may, eventually, lead to job mobility in the United States.

My findings, then, are in harmony with those of other studies claim that legal status does not have a direct effect on labor market outcomes (Massey 1987b; Bailey 1985). What appears to be more important is its indirect effect via job security and time spent in the United States. Most important, though, are the immigrant job networks which, better than anything else, explain the labor market outcomes of the Maya in Houston.

Deserving of future study is the question of how legalization influences the employment and wage situation of undocumented newcomers. While we have not systematically examined this among the Maya community, conversations with legalized members of the community and calls from legalized members looking for jobs for newcomer relatives suggest that it is taking longer for newcomers to find jobs.

⚤ INCREASED INTERACTION BETWEEN HOUSTON AND TOTONICAPAN

Almost every new legal resident in the community has gone home to visit San Pedro at least once; most make the trip several times a year. The legal status of the temporary resident allows one to travel outside the United States for a period of up to one month. With permanent resident status, this period is extended to six months. For many immigrants this is the greatest short-term benefit of the program and, for some, it became the principal motivation for applying for the second stage of legalization, permanent residence. Recall that in the end, most of the Maya applied as a short-term strategy to buy time to earn money once they saw the ease with which they could get temporary resident status and the advantages of this status. Similarly, as the community watched others pass easily through the English requirements (most opted for the classes, not the exam) and most important, saw the first members visit their families in San Pedro, more of the Maya applied for legalization, not with the intention of permanently settling in the United States, but for the freedom to travel between the two countries. I shall now describe some community members' impressions of their visits back home, and then show how interaction between the two communities has been strengthened as a result of the legalization program.

Pablo related the following comments to me after his second trip home since receiving his temporary residency card:

> I really enjoyed it, even more this time. I had intended to do a lot of traveling with my new truck, but we [his wife and child] spent most of the time with family, especially with my mother-in-law. María [his wife] spent a lot of time showing Belinda [their daughter] how to prepare foods and taking her around the village. I watched a lot of cable TV with relatives [one of the many appliances he brought back with him] and playing soccer. No, I don't think I could ever go back and live there, even though I really enjoy it. I am too used to life in Houston, and it would be especially hard for my daughters there.

Julio, the young entrepreneur who entered the courier business, spoke about how he was treated when he went home for the first time:

> They acted differently with me. They called me a Ladino in Quiché and treated me differently than before. Espe-

cially in the church. When I told the church elders about the work I was doing here in my church [he is an instructor of Bible classes at a Seventh Day Adventist church] they asked me to talk to the people one day at church.

It was apparent from the manner in which Julio related his experience that he enjoyed his new status, especially as it pertained to religious events back home.

As I mentioned above, many of his Houston friends believe that, once he finds a wife in Guatemala, he will return to Houston and become a permanent resident. In fact, they have a running bet on this.

Interestingly, legal status appears to have indirectly influenced Julio's social status back home by allowing him to return home more often. By taking capital earned in the States and reinvesting it in the local economy in the form of property, and by earning the prestige of the church elders, he has improved his social status in San Pedro. Julio is one of many in the Houston community who are investing in Totonicapán—in the form of property, higher education for children, renovations on existing homes, and such entrepreneurial activities as bakeries and tailoring businesses.

Another migrant, a young single man in his early twenties, passed along the following impressions:

> It was good going home. It got rid of that feeling. You know, that feeling that grows when you're away too long; like you've got to go back. Now I'm not so anxious to return forever. I don't need to. I can go whenever I want with my green card and still live here. It will be like having two homes.

Monica, one of the few, single women to obtain legal status, discussed her changing perceptions and intentions after her first visit home in six years.

The best part was being with my family, especially my mother and sisters. Cooking with them, just talking. I can't wait to go again. Yes, there were some difficult moments. It's a hard life there. Women spend all their time in the kitchen. Everything takes hours. I was most happy about bringing home a blender and other kitchen things for my mother. I felt different somehow. I think they saw me differently too. My mother was very upset about my hair [she recently had her hairstyle modernized]. She didn't say so, but my sister told me she was. It's hard being a woman there now that I have lived here. I'm not saying it's not hard here, because it is. I work six days a week and sometimes seven, but at least I have opportunities here, especially now that I am learning English. My family wants me eventually to go home, but I don't know. They don't understand my feelings about it at all. The only opportunity for a woman there is through marriage and I am thirty-one. You can be thirty-one and not married here and it's okay, like you. It's harder there. I don't know. I really miss my mother, but I really want a good job and want to meet a man. Maybe it will be easier here once I learn English. I'd like to bring my other sisters here once I get permanent residency, especially since Herma can't go back. [Her only sister in the United States could not apply for amnesty because she had been picked up on two occasions by INS when trying to cross the border. Both instances occurred after the legalization cutoff date for applicants.] I know my parents would never come. It would be too much of a change. Yet how can I take my sisters away from them?

The above comments illustrate the social and cultural distance that return immigrants feel when they go back home. All sensed they had been gone too long and had grown accustomed to the United States. For the women, the hardest aspect of returning home to Guatemala, even for a visit, is the rigid Maya normative structure governing social relations. In her study of Dominican women in New York City, Pessar (1982, 1986) also found that women, because of the subordinate role they assume, were more likely than men to voice hesitancy about returning home. Women returning home spend most of their time in the household with their families—caring for children, cooking, and cleaning. While they are expected to reassume their traditional roles, the men experience greater freedom and are treated with elevated respect by members of the home community. As my fellow researcher, Nestor Rodríguez, commented, upon returning from his most recent trip to Guatemala:

> Once the women return home, they find themselves spending most of the day inside, assisting other women with domestic duties and caring for the children. Meanwhile, the men are driving around the countryside in their newly purchased trucks, visiting friends and kin and relating success stories of Houston. Yes, I heard some criticism of women who were not wearing their *traje* [traditional garments worn by Maya women].

For most of the newly legalized members of the community, especially the young women, returning home impressed upon them the advantages of settling in Houston. Yet, not all were willing to say they would never go back on a permanent basis. They don't need to. Their new "green card" has the paradoxical effect of providing them with geographic mobility: they can travel to and from Guatemala as often as they like.

By providing for legal return migration, the legalization program promotes greater community-level interaction between San Pedro and Houston, thereby reinforcing and expanding an established network infrastructure. The trip home is no longer restricted to a few brave undocumented migrants;

return visits en masse of some fifty newly legalized Maya can take place. Indeed, most of the Maya do not make the trip alone, but drive to Guatemala with friends and kin.

There are also particular community holidays and events that reunite the Houston community with San Pedro. Having the freedom to travel back and forth, more and more legalized Maya are returning to Guatemala to participate in such events. These include the July Fiesta de Santiago, Christmas, and Easter. The observer of daily life in the Houston community sees an emerging pattern. Weeks before these events take place immigrants begin preparing for the trip home. The preparations involve 1. locating another person in the community to replace oneself at work (very common and manageable with the tight job networks among the men and women); 2. locating another community member to take care of those children who do not have legal status; 3. visiting with friends and relatives who wish to send money and other items with the returning migrant; and 4. purchasing clothing and other consumer goods to be taken as gifts to family and friends in Guatemala.

Organizational linkages between the two communities have also been created or strengthened through legalization. Return migration to San Pedro helped to reactivate a soccer team in Houston and to organize intercommunity sports events between Houston and San Pedro. Legal status, remember, motivated members of the soccer team to reach out to a neighborhood community organization for assistance with the formation of a soccer league. Shortly after the Houston team reestablished itself, it began planning for a match against the home team in San Pedro. One of my informants recently returned from a month-long trip to San Pedro, where he attended the intercommunity match. He reported seeing at least forty faces from the Houston community, and returned with a videotape of the match to show to the Houston

community. Consistent with the longitudinal research conducted by Massey and colleagues (1987), my study finds that
voluntary community organizations, such as soccer teams,
can support the reintegration of the returning Maya in Guatemala and can provide a forum for the periodic exchange of news
between the home community and migrants living in Houston.

Organizational linkages were also formed between health
workers in Houston and San Pedro as a result of legalization.
Recall that the Maya had reached out to a group of Anglos to
assist in collecting medical supplies for a health clinic in San
Pedro. The group, Amigos de San Pedro, accompanied a
group of migrants returning to San Pedro. Armed with equipment, medicine, and funds, the two groups made their way to
Guatemala in the summer of 1992. The Anglo members of
the contingent were recognized and honored by a municipal
committee in Totonicapán as well as by the Guatemalan
community in Houston. Shortly before their departure for
Guatemala, several residents of the Houston Maya community collected and put aside funds to provide for two meals a day
for the visiting group of Anglos. In Totonicapán the Anglo
visitors stayed in a house built by means of remittances from
one of the Maya men living in Houston.

Once in the community of Totonicapán, the Anglo contingent was rewarded for its efforts with dinners, a luncheon
at the mayor's office, hand-painted certificates of appreciation, and a silver plaque engraved with words of appreciation.
At the annual fiesta, the mayor and other municipal representatives, in the presence of the entire township, publicly
thanked their Anglo friends from Houston for all their help.

The reactivation of the soccer team and subsequent development of intercommunity soccer games, along with the
establishment of health-care exchanges between the two
communities, represent the growth of new organizational
linkages between the communities as a result of legalization.

Thus, it is safe to conclude that legalization has strengthened international ties between the two communities by building networks beyond the household level.

The presence of many newly legalized immigrants in return visits to Guatemala also stimulates migration to Houston. As recently legalized immigrants return home and tell friends, kin, and other Maya about life in Houston, new migrants make their way north. Since the first wave of newly legalized immigrants returned to Guatemala, researchers working in the field have detected an increase in migration from San Pedro to Houston. When the fieldwork began in the summer of 1986, the Totonicapán Maya in Houston numbered about one thousand; since then, the community has swelled to more than two thousand. Returning migrants can assure the home community about work they thought was no longer available as a result of employer sanctions. Moreover, the knowledge that relatives in Houston are applying for permanent residence, and will soon be able to sponsor family members back home, also stimulates some to make the move north.

The Houston Maya community now includes undocumented as well as legal residents. Increasingly, too, households comprise persons of various statuses. Interestingly, this differentiation has not resulted in noticeable community stratification (except that between undocumented women and their male legalized partners). The legal Maya live and work alongside their undocumented counterparts. Clearly, though, opportunities are greater for those who have job security and the freedom to travel to and from Guatemala. An interesting research question for the future is whether these opportunities, if and when they translate into social mobility, will eventually create differences in life chances and well-being among the Maya community in Houston.

CHAPTER SIX

CONCLUSION

THE CENTRAL STORY OF THIS BOOK HAS BEEN THE
settlement experience of an undocumented Maya community in
the context of major immigration policy reform. I have structured this story chronologically, beginning with the arrival of
the first Maya pioneer in Houston, then moving to the development of a viable Maya community in the city and to the
acquisition of legal status by community members. By structuring the story in this way I have been able to show the importance
of studying undocumented settlement as a process and of understanding immigration reform as it unfolds in the community. In
this concluding chapter, we move beyond the Maya narrative to
explore the larger implications of their story for migration
theory and research and for immigration policy making.

☗ MIGRATION THEORY AND RESEARCH: THEMATIC OBSERVATIONS FROM THE MAYA CASE

Embedded in this book are four major themes that, I
believe, transcend the legalization story and consequently

have wider implications for immigration theory and research. These include 1. the role of social networks in facilitating settlement and regulating migration; 2. the differential settlement experience of women and men; 3. the complexity and heterogeneity of decision making with respect to migrant settlement plans; and 4. the evolving social relations between home and host communities.

Migrant Networks

Early in the study, I asked each of the seventy-four Maya in the sample why they left Guatemala to come to the United States. Not surprisingly, almost all the responses centered on perceptions of greater economic opportunity. Some cited a "lack of jobs back home"; others emphasized "the need to earn money to help pay for the children's education in Guatemala." Most, however, spoke of "higher wages" in the United States.

When asked why they selected Houston, rather than some other place in the United States, all responded that they came to Houston because they knew someone living in the city who was from their hometown, either a family member or a friend. Similarly, when asked how they found a place to live and a place to work, they spoke of friends and family who provided housing and access to jobs. Indeed, in most cases, the newcomers knew with whom they would be living and where they would be working prior to their arrival.

As the Maya responses show, and as others have repeatedly found in other migrant communities, economic considerations drive the decision to migrate; once that decision is made, though, migration increasingly develops into a social process (Macdonald and Macdonald 1974; Lomnitz 1977; Roberts 1974; Massey et al. 1987). The pioneer migrant, for whatever idiosyncratic reason, chooses a place to settle. Juan, the pioneer of the Houston Maya community, had heard of the city in Guatemala and decided it would be the first place to look for a job. The pioneer then brings over those closest to him from the home community. Juan's two brothers-in-law, his wife, and his children were the first Maya to join him. This is the initial network in the migrant community. Once established in the host community, each person in this embryonic network reaches out to others in the home community, who then become potential migrants. Juan found jobs for kin and close friends, while Carmen assisted in recruiting the first cohort of women to Houston. In the home community, word spreads concerning the success of these early and adventurous pioneers; the motivation to migrate builds. What is interesting in the Maya case, in contrast to Mexican migrant communities, is that for several years no return migration was necessary to trigger more migration from the home community; that is, the earliest pioneers did not return to Guatemala until many years later, after the Maya had established themselves in Houston.

Over time, the migrant community grows in size as these networks reach out from the immediate family to incorporate other kin and eventually anyone from the home community. Over a period of years, even neighboring communities are networked in to the migration process. In the case of the Maya, the networks from San Pedro reached out to incorporate many communities in the Department of Totonicapán. These networks grow in strength and resiliency as the migrants adapt to the new conditions and demands of the host society (Massey et al. 1987). Thus, the neighborhood networks, housing networks, and job networks develop. With the establishment of these now multiple, overlapping networks, the costs of migration for the newcomer Maya are reduced as they increasingly arrive in the new community with access to a rich array of social resources. These include initial housing, job referrals, and information about how to get along in the host society. Besides the interpersonal networks that help newcomers in the initial stages of settlement,

the development of voluntary organizations further strength-
ens and reinforces network relations in the host community
(Massey et al. 1987). In the case of the Maya community in
Houston, the development of a community church, intergroup health clinic, and several soccer teams reinforced established networks and served as vehicles for constant
community interaction. Over time, these social networks
linking families, households, and communities serve to sustain migration from the home community. My findings are
consistent with those of others who argue that international
migration becomes a self-sustaining social process, irrespec-
tive of public policies (e.g., IRCA) that try to regulate it
(Donato et al. 1992). In fact, our research suggests that IRCA
has actually facilitated further migration from the home community, as newly legalized migrants returned with their stories of success in Houston. This emerging pattern will be
elaborated on below.

The Totonicapán Maya community in Houston has been
quite successful, relative to many other immigrant populations in the city, in adapting to a new culture and society. We
attribute their success to the strength of their social networks
(Rodríguez 1987; Rodríguez and Hagan 1989). One area in
which the Totonicapán Maya have been strikingly successful
is the rate at which they legalized, despite the fact that many
were technically ineligible. This can largely be explained by
the strength of their social networks, which circulated information on how the process worked and what the benefits of
participation would be.

The resources of the personal-based networks of the Maya
community, however, did not guarantee a successful petition.
Their main benefits were reaped during the first stage of the
legalization process—decision making—when they were the
means of disseminating information on "how to legalize" and
were conduits for sharing "legalization experiences." This
study found that during the second stage of legalization—

collecting documentation—applicants also depended on established residents (e.g., coworkers, neighbors), outside of their social networks, to supply the affidavits necessary to assure a successful application.

In his work on the relationship between social mobility and networks, Granovetter (1973) demonstrates the importance of distinguishing between "strong ties"—those found in relationships between family and close friends—and "weak ties"—those found in relationships between acquaintances. According to Granovetter, weak ties maximize opportunities because they bridge different groups, thereby maximizing the flow of information. Applying Granovetter's distinctions to the settlement experience of the Maya in Houston, my research found the role of personal-based networks to be the most important during the initial stage of settlement by providing the newcomer with social resources such as housing, transportation, access to information, and general information about U.S. culture and society. For the more established migrant—intergroup relationships, those with established residents—become increasingly important because they facilitate opportunities to formally settle in the receiving society, that is, in becoming legal. These findings suggest that future research on social networks and migration should devote more attention to the dynamics of social networks, especially conditions under which they weaken (Boyd 1989).

Gender and Settlement

The Maya community is a relatively homogeneous group. Its members share ethnicity and language, class background, and community of origin. However, in one very important way the community is split: gender. The migratory and settlement experiences of women and men are quite different. Some of the most ambitious and comprehensive longitudinal studies of immigrant settlement (Massey et al. 1987; Portes and Bach 1985) have missed this important difference, either by not considering women in their studies or by assuming that women's experiences resemble those of men.

My study finds that gender differences run through the entire migration experience, beginning with the journey to the United States. The financial and social costs of making the trip are much higher for women than for men. The men in the community usually travel to the United States in small groups; in most cases, they travel by bus to Mexico and then hire a "coyote" to take them across the U.S.-Mexico border. The average cost of the trip is approximately five hundred dollars.

For obvious reasons of safety, the women are reluctant to travel alone or in the exclusive company of women. Moreover, many of the male migrants are reluctant to travel with women because to do so is more complicated. The Maya women, especially those who are single, are forced to rely on two coyotes (one to take them across the Guatemala-Mexico border, the other to take them across the U.S.-Mexico border). On average, a woman pays twelve hundred dollars in coyote fees, over twice the amount paid by her male counterpart. In many cases, the coyote retains the woman's identification papers until her final payment is made, which can take up to a year in some cases, leaving her truly undocumented in both the United States and Guatemala.

Once the migrants arrive in the United States, these gender differences are perpetuated; for, once here, the Maya women find themselves embedded in networks that are neither the same as nor equal to those of men. Basically, the women's networks are weaker and far less extensive. Arriving in the 1980s, the women encountered a burgeoning demand for private domestic work, owing to the increasing participation in the labor force of women with children (Chafetz 1990). While Maya women and men both use community-based social networks to locate jobs, it takes the women much longer to find an initial job and, once they land the job, the remuneration is much lower than that earned by the men. Because the men control recruitment, newcomer men find jobs rapidly. Moreover, those of the Houston community work for a rapidly growing company of supermarkets, each of which has teams of Maya workers through whom newcomers gain access to jobs. In contrast, women rely on the casual and informal conversations that pass between employers and their domestics. The weaker job networks for women, and the size of their workplace, usually mean that they take much longer than their male counterparts to land a job. Women often wait months before finding a job. Moreover, in the formal sector of the labor market, entry-level workers earn minimum wage, while most employers of live-in domestics are willing to pay a starting salary of only a hundred dollars a week for five to six days (and often evenings) of work.

Once the job is located, the female migrant then experiences a dramatic shift in her living arrangements, moving from the relative comfort of the immigrant neighborhood to the isolation of a bedroom in her employer's house. Her contact with the Maya community is restricted to one weekend day in the neighborhood and to church meetings and the occasional community celebration of life-cycle events, such as weddings. In contrast, the men interact daily—in the neighborhood, at the workplace, during soccer practices and games, and just hanging out or working on their cars. Thus, women's community-based networks are less extensive, and their contact with established residents is more restricted than men's. Ultimately, as the period of settlement increased, the Maya social networks became gendered.

The implications for women's settlement opportunities are several. In our case, it meant that women were forced to rely on one employer for the documentation needed to legalize. Because most employers of domestics refused to provide such documentation, for fear of IRS reprisal for not paying social security, only a handful of domestics secured legal status—this despite the fact that many in the larger Totonicapán community were eligible, having arrived before 1982. Moreover, of the nine women in the study sample who did acquire legal status, seven were married and four worked as day domestics. Being married and working for several employers allowed them to reach out further for assistance in obtaining documentation. The single women were definitely disadvantaged. Recall the tragic story of Sonya. Unable to secure an affidavit from her employer, even though she was eligible for legal status, Sonya roamed through the neighborhood, going door-to-door, looking for a familiar face who would help her.

Even though many of the single women did not succeed in obtaining legal status, and although many of the married women have become increasingly dependent on their husbands to eventually obtain it, migration does appear to provide some opportunities for women. It is just that the opportunities appear to come more slowly for women than for men. Most women in the community cite first-time wage employment as the greatest benefit of migration. Unlike many of the men, who use their discretionary income to buy cars and to other material goods, women sent home most of their earned income to supplement family income and to help with their children's education. Most women believe that, with time, their earnings will enable them to free up some discretionary cash so that they can also invest in transportation and education. Interestingly, the women seem more committed than the men to learning English, evidenced in the fact that more women are enrolled in English classes. Moreover, their employers encourage and support this step, as it enables better communication with the domestic. Many of the Maya women believe that English may be the key skill that takes the Maya women out of the domestic industry and into the formal economy.

Women's participation in the informal sector may also

protect them from the employer sanctions provision of IRCA. If and when employer sanctions ever have a real impact on the hiring practices of undocumented workers in Houston's formal labor market, the men will be at a disadvantage. The undocumented domestics may be protected, since INS has made it clear it will not actively seek out employers of such domestics. Thus, there is an irony in this story: while women's labor market participation as domestics has limited their participation in the legalization program, it may ultimately protect them from losing their jobs and being deported.

In their comprehensive review of studies on migration and gender, Tienda and Booth (1991) also highlight the mixed bag of opportunities and constraints that women face as a result of migration. Migration does provide previously unemployed women with the opportunity to earn income that, over time, may increase autonomy and lead to further opportunities. On the other hand, these benefits of migration may never develop so long as women remain in an unregulated industry that pays poorly and offers little opportunity for social mobility, except day domestic work.

In sum, my research shows that the opportunities provided by IRCA have not benefited many of the women in the Houston Maya community. It is highly probable that this pattern exists in other migrant communities in the United States as well, given the concentration of migrant women in domestic work, especially in places like Houston and Washington, D.C. where service jobs predominate (Hagan 1989; Repak 1994). Moreover, since women constitute an increasing proportion of the migrant flows to this country, the study's findings suggest a need for more comprehensive research on the social structures (e.g., gendered social networks) that dictate the differential settlement experiences and opportunities of male and female migrants (Grasmuck and Pessar 1991). Moreover, the finding that women, because of their labor market position and work conditions, were less

likely to legalize than were men, indicates that the legalization provision of IRCA, was, as Boyd suggests that many of the
immigration policies are, "explicitly formulated and implemented on the presumption of males as breadwinners and
females as dependent spouses" (Boyd 1989:659).

Decision Making and Settlement

Perhaps no other dimension of my research was as difficult to
conceptualize as the migrant decision-making process as it
relates to settlement plans and the acquisition of legal status.
The difficulty of pinpointing the factors influencing a migrant's decision to settle formally in the United States stems
from the temporal and informal character of undocumented
migration. The precarious and clandestine nature of undocumented life, with its constant ambiguity, discourages the
migrant from making long-term plans. Thus, decision making
evolves into a continual process, whereby decisions shift with
changing sets of opportunities, attitudes, and social relations
in both the home and the host community. Even as I write, I
know that most of the Maya with legal status have yet to
commit themselves to permanent settlement in the United
States, not to mention U.S. citizenship.

From the moment of their decision to depart Guatemala
to the present day, the Maya migrants have been rational
actors, but their decisions have been based on short- to
medium-term considerations. This is entirely consistent with
undocumented behavior, which constantly adapts to envi-
ronmental opportunities. At the community level, the decision to legalize can be understood best as a rational, adaptive
strategy that bought increasing amounts of time to work in
this country. The decision was converted into action by
means of the circulation of information through the migrant
networks.

Opportunities also vary with the status of the individual.
The most relevant factors are time in the United States,

gender, marital status and, for the married, the residence of spouse and children (i.e., in Houston or in Guatemala). These statuses affect migrant decision making because they influence not only the opportunities the migrants experience but, equally important, their perceptions and expectations. When one acknowledges the importance of each of these statuses on the decision-making process, it becomes clear that migrant choices not only make sense individually but as observable, patterned behavior.

Those who were firmest in their decision to apply for legal status and who remain fairly certain that they will seek naturalization are married couples with children who have lived in Houston for several years. Repeatedly, the children's welfare, especially their education, is cited as the most important factor influencing the decision to settle permanently in the United States. Parents who have children in Guatemala, however, remain indecisive, arguing that their settlement plans will depend on whether their children join them in the United States. Children represent community roots, and the longer they live in a community the deeper the family's roots there, regardless of whether the parents actually live with the children at every moment.

For the young single members of the community, the "roots" theme does not emerge. What does emerge, however, are gender differences in motivation to legalize and in long-term settlement plans. For the great majority of young single men in the community, the motives that drove their application to legalize were short-term practical considerations. A legalization petition brought them immediate work authorization. Thus, their petitions can best be understood as a temporary survival strategy: it bought more time to work and earn money. Ultimately, Maya men—newcomers and established alike—in the Houston community express long-term plans to return eventually to Guatemala.

The decision-making process for the young single women

in the community is a bit more complicated, as it appears to be especially influenced by time in the United States. While several works have found that newcomers are more likely than their established counterparts to voice intentions of return migration, only recently have studies highlighted gen-der differences (Grasmuck and Pessar 1991). I found that female newcomers, feeling isolated from the Maya communi-ty in both Guatemala and the United States, are very likely to see their stay in Houston as temporary and to express inten-tions of returning home to Guatemala. In contrast, the more established female migrants are motivated to settle in the United States; they feel socially distant from women in the Guatemalan home community. That is to say, the longer they stay here, the more aware these single women become of the social and economic advantages their sex has in the United States, compared with Maya society in Guatemala. Men, on the other hand, regardless of the settlement period, express intentions of returning.

Much of the past research focusing on decision making in relation to changing legal status has been cross-sectional in nature, and consequently it has not been possible to distin-guish motivations from expectations or post-factum rational-izations (Portes and Truelove 1987). My findings demonstrate that decision making should be studied as a process if we are to pinpoint actual motivations and distinguish the various stages that are involved in decision making. Further, research must move beyond an individual focus to investigate why immigrants decide to legalize. My research suggests not only that motivations vary by marital status and gender, but that the strength and nature of community social networks also have a strong influence on the decision-making process.

Evolving Relations between the Houston and Guatemalan Communities

Yet another important theme that has emerged in this study is the role of legalization in enhancing social ties between the

Guatemalan home community and the Maya community in Houston. Legalization has strengthened these ties because of two outcomes—one intended by the national-policy framers of IRCA, the other an unintended consequence that can be understood only from the community's perspective.

Legal status provides an opportunity to strengthen social and economic ties to the host society. Policymakers should not be surprised by this development, as it was anticipated that many immigrants would use legal status as a device to integrate into various aspects of U.S. society (e.g., economic protection in the labor market, increased interaction with U.S. culture and institutions). However, equally meaningful, yet probably far more surprising to IRCA's framers, is the reality that legalized immigrants are simultaneously reintegrating into their home communities.

Prior to acquiring legal status, formerly undocumented migrants in the community ruled out visits to Guatemala because of the risks. The trip to Guatemala's western highlands was a long and arduous one, and the return to the United States was equally difficult, risking apprehension at the U.S. border. This has all changed with IRCA. With legal residence, the formerly undocumented Maya can, for the first time, visit their home villages without jeopardizing their ability to live and work in Houston. With permanent residence status, they can remain in Guatemala for a period of six months—and that is exactly what several of the Maya are doing.

Most of the legalized Maya have made several trips home, usually for holidays and special events. Some, however, are actually living in Guatemala for as much as six months a year, returning to the States to have their passports stamped and to buy various goods to sell back in their home villages, then returning home for another six-month period. Still others are part of a different settlement pattern, making the United States their home base but returning to Guatemala for visits, often investing in property and business back home. Still

others, like Julio the courier, have returned to live in Guatemala, but regularly return to the United States for business.
The long-term settlement outcomes of these group migratory
patterns remain unclear. Binational residence could be a transi-
tional process; that is, it may be limited to the first generation of
legalized persons, and not necessarily be reproduced among the
sons and daughters of these newly legalized persons.

In contrast, the undocumented members of the Houston
Maya community voice greater fear than ever of returning
home for a visit and being apprehended at the U.S. border.
They hope one day to acquire legal status through a legalized
family member or through another legalization program. Thus,
one of the most fascinating and unanticipated outcomes of
IRCA may be the creation of a cohort of "permanent" legal
residents who are, paradoxically, more geographically mobile
than their undocumented counterparts (Hagan and Baker
1993). Having "permanent" residence, then, allows the migrant to keep his or her settlement options open.

In the long run, migration under "permanent" residence
status may assume the temporary features of undocumented
Mexican migration and legal Puerto Rican flows, ultimately
leading to a binational residence pattern among "permanent"
residents. In the past, we have assumed that this temporal
feature was distinctive among undocumented immigrants
working in seasonal jobs in agriculture (Baca and Bryan
1983). But my findings suggest that this temporary rhythm
may also emerge among immigrants working in urban industrial areas.

This unanticipated migratory pattern suggests that we
must reexamine, even respecify, two aspects of the migration
process. First, such concepts as "permanent" and "temporary"
migration must be respecified in light of these new, post-IRCA
contexts. Permanent residence may describe a legal status,

but the social reality of immigrant behavior may reflect permanent and temporary aspects of settlement. Second, the adjustment to legal status of a previously undocumented community may strengthen rather than weaken international social ties. The legalized immigrant cohort, that group with the longest record of U.S. residence which had firm ties to U.S. communities, is the same group of people who first sought the opportunity to visit and invest in their home villages in the country of origin (Hagan and Baker 1993).

Further evidence suggesting a strengthening, rather than a weakening of ties between the Houston and Guatemalan communities is the expansion of voluntary organizational links between the two (e.g., the reactivation of the soccer teams) and an observed increase in new migration from the home community to Houston. Since IRCA, as mentioned earlier, the Houston community has doubled in number, swelling to over two thousand. This new migratory cohort consists of returnees (i.e., those who had left Houston early in IRCA's implementation) and new members from many neighboring communities in the western highlands of Guatemala who remain confident that they can find jobs in the United States. This confidence is not unfounded. Employer sanctions have not had any impact on the job security of undocumented Maya in Houston. Moreover, fraudulent documentation for entering the U.S. labor market is easily accessible to migrants in the city. Most important, though, is the fact that legalized members have a strong foothold in the U.S. labor market, thus providing continued access to jobs for prospective undocumented migrants from Guatemala. In sum, legalization continues to engender changes in the immigrant community that both encourage continued migration and strengthen, possibly even expand, international social networks.

166 ～ **DECIDING TO BE LEGAL**

♔♔ IMMIGRATION POLICY MAKING: LESSONS FROM THE FIELD

The central goal of IRCA was to halt the flow of undocumented migrants to the United States. It relied on three complementary approaches to reach its objective. First, it imposed
penalties on employers who hired unauthorized workers. Secondly, it increased the resources available to INS for border
enforcement by 50 percent of its operating budget (Bean et
al. 1989). Finally, it provided two main paths to permanent
residence: 1. a one-shot general legalization program for
undocumented workers who had been living in the country
since January 1, 1982 and 2. a special legalization program for
undocumented migrants who had worked as agricultural la-
borers for at least ninety days during 1986.

The studies that have dominated the post-IRCA research
agenda have focused on the effects of IRCA on the flow of
undocumented Mexican migration to the United States. The
results are in. The overwhelming bulk of these studies conclude that IRCA has had a weak to negligible effect on curtail-
ing undocumented migration to the United States (Bean et
al. 1990b; Donato et al. 1992; Massey et al. 1990).

Even when we simply rely on questionable INS arrest data,
the pattern is clear.[1] The U.S. border patrol and other INS
personnel apprehended a high of 1.8 million illegal aliens in
1986. There was a short drop in arrests in 1988 and 1989,
suggesting that perhaps IRCA was working. This post-1986
drop in arrests, however, could be partially a result of the
general and agricultural legalization programs of IRCA. Together, these programs provided legal documentation to roughly 3 million formerly undocumented persons who otherwise
may have tried to cross the border illegally (Bean et al. 1989).
Since 1989, the number of arrests has been increasing steadily, which strongly suggests that IRCA has done little to alter

the basic pattern of undocumented migration to the United States.

Two research and policy questions emerge here. First, why has U.S. immigration policy, embodied in IRCA, failed to regulate the flow of undocumented migrants to the United States and their entry into the U.S. labor market? Second, is immigration policy the arena in which we should continue attempting to control undocumented labor migration, or are there other policies that could be more effective? Let us now address these questions by critically examining each of IRCA's central approaches to reducing undocumented migration.

To answer the first question we must recognize that one of IRCA's provisions, legalization, worked. There are lessons to be had from the legalization experience—lessons that may both help to explain the relative failure of IRCA's other central provision, employer sanctions, and help to inform the future design and implementation of U.S. immigration policy. Legalization worked because it responded and adapted to the needs and realities of undocumented life. By providing immediate benefits (work authorization) INS played into the settlement strategies of undocumented immigrants. Moreover, legalization engendered changes in immigrant communities that appear to encourage continued migration and strengthen international social networks (Hagan and Baker 1993). Other studies also find that IRCA has increased the flow of migrants, especially women and children joining their newly legalized family member (González de la Rocha and Escobar Latapí 1990; Cornelius 1989).

The employer sanctions provision makes it very easy for the employer to follow the letter of the law without carrying out the spirit of the law. The provision requires that each employer have all new employees fill out I-9 forms and provide proof of work authorization. Various Labor Department–sponsored field studies (including one in which I was involved in Houston) found that, indeed, employers are well informed about the law and are requesting that all new employees provide the required documentation. Similarly, unauthorized workers are aware of the need to present documents to obtain employment. The problem, however, is that most unauthorized workers also know how to obtain fraudulent documents that are virtually indistinguishable from legitimate ones (Hagan 1989; Rodríguez 1989b; Repak 1989; Loucky and Chinchilla 1989). Thus, employers are complying with the law so long as they collect the documentation, fraudulent or not. Moreover, INS has not been entirely committed to investigating fraudulent documents in the workplace.

Employer sanctions appear to have failed for other reasons as well. The law never really shifted the burden of proof from the worker to the employer. The only way to make employer sanctions work is for government to put more resources into employer enforcement. Clearly, it is not in the interest of government to do this. Federal funding for such enforcement has waned, and the employer certainly gets nothing out of it. Should we be so surprised by this policy outcome? Heavy-handed government interference in the business sector contradicts the basic principles of the free-enterprise system. Moreover, can we really expect immigration policy to regulate the labor supply of a free-market system in which employers have historically depended on international labor?

Another reason for the failure of employer sanctions is that the law is not responsive to the realities of how work is socially organized. Undocumented immigrants gain access to the workplace through social networks, and, as the Maya men show, sometimes they even control the recruitment process. All that employer sanctions have done is to delay such access for the time it takes to acquire fraudulent documentation for those employers who require it (Hagan 1989; Rodríguez 1989b). Newcomers clearly face a more complicated labor market now that documents are required for employment. As a result, more than ever, newcomers must rely on informal social networks to obtain documents (Bach and Brill 1989). Once again, the theme of social networks emerges. The stronger the social network to which the immigrant is connected, the greater the opportunity to work, regardless of policies that try to regulate such behavior.

As a nation, we have exhausted our patience with sanctions as a policy tool. The only remaining enforcement-based alternative is border monitoring, and that is exactly where we have turned. At the time of this writing, "Operation Blockade," a federally funded border-monitoring project, is under way in the El Paso, Texas, area of the U.S.-Mexico border. Moreover, the U.S. border patrol, with the aid of military personnel, is currently in the planning stage of erecting ten-foot-high chain-link fences along the U.S.-Mexico border in El Paso, Arizona, and southern California (Pinkerton 1993). By increasing funds for staffing the area with U.S. border patrol personnel and by erecting a fence along the border, the U.S. government attempts to appease worried citizens in these areas.

In the short run, this strategy may work for a concentrated area along the border. In the long run, though, it will no doubt fail. For one thing, the U.S. government may well be propelled to implement a public relations stunt in order to show the public that it is doing something about undocumented migration. Such a strategy, moreover, is not politically viable; it is too controversial. After all, how can we militarize a border at the same time we are opening up our borders via the North American Free-Trade Agreement (NAFTA)? Through the signing and passage of NAFTA into law, we have made a commitment to further globalization of our economy. Are we not contradicting such a commitment to our neighbors south of the border by further militarizing the border?

If, as a nation, we do not want to militarize the border and do not want to spend vast sums of money regulating U.S. employers, the only other option is to revamp the benefits system so that the supply of visas and the demand for entry into the United States mesh better. This is clearly what we tried to do in IRCA and, most recently, in the Immigration Act of 1990. With legalization, or "amnesty," the United States provided benefits to unskilled workers to meet the demands of the market. Legalization worked, but as a continued policy tool it is unrealistic. How can we provide legalization over and over again? With the Immigration Act of 1990 we responded to the market's perception of a demand for skilled labor by providing an annual increase in legal employment based immigration. This most recent strategy, while yet another short-term response to market demands, does little to solve the problem of migrant flows of unskilled workers. Ultimately, what we are left with is the continued flow of people who are trying to make a better living.

Thus, until the Maya can make a better living in their home communities, or in places other than Houston, the social process of migration will sustain the flow to the Houston labor market. U.S. immigration policies that try to regulate migrant entry and access to jobs have been largely ineffective, for community networks have clearly adapted to and overcome such constraints. There is little that immigration policy can do to regulate such a flow.

It is perhaps time that we rely less on immigration policy to regulate labor migration and more on mutual- and regional-development policies that decrease the motivation to migrate in the first place. If and when NAFTA is eventually extended to Central America and South America, trade policy may be the first step toward sustained development in these countries. Such trade-linked development strategies are actually only a formal legitimation of what many of the Maya are already doing—reinvesting in their communities of origin, increasing social and economic exchanges between the two communities. Free-trade-linked development and additional foreign and domestic investment in Guatemala may be the only viable way for the Guatemalan economy to create jobs and thereby reduce unskilled-worker migration to the United States. Opponents of this argument claim that so long as wage differentials exist between the two economies, migration will persist. The European experience, however, tells a different story. Most studies of the European Community countries have found that economic integration in Western Europe has not had the effect of triggering large-scale migration from the poorer regions to the more affluent (Piper and Reynolds 1991). Recent studies of the relationship between NAFTA and Mexican immigration also conclude that, in the long run, NAFTA will create jobs for rural Mexican workers, thereby reducing Mexican rural migration to the United States (Cornelius and Martin 1993).

For the Totonicapán Maya, remember, migration is primarily a strategy to increase their chances for economic mobility. In the absence of this motivating factor, most of the Maya from Totonicapán would clearly prefer to stay in their home communities, with family and friends and in a familiar culture. Migration is a costly strategy, but by relying on social networks to pursue this strategy, the Maya reduce some of the financial and social costs associated with leaving one's home and settling in a new country. Without economic opportunities in the western highland villages of Totonicapán, Maya migration to Houston will likely persist, despite immigration policies that try to restrict such movement. However, if economic conditions in these home communities were to improve, or if a different set of opportunities were to emerge, it is very possible that the Maya networks would adapt to these changing conditions, either by maturing to a stable level or by reorganizing and moving in a new direction.

NOTES

1. Various terms have been used to refer to the Maya. Some anthropologists use the term "Indian," especially when speaking of the Maya in Guatemala (Smith 1990; Adams 1990). I refrain from using this term, as it is considered derogatory by the San Pedro Totonicapán community in Houston. To complicate the issue further, *within* the community, the Totonicapán Maya refer to themselves as *naturales*, but in the company of non-Maya they use the term *indígenas*. The former term translates into "naturals"; the latter term to "indigenous." For the non-Maya reader, neither term makes much sense, especially when referring to the Maya outside their native land. This leaves us with the term "Maya," which has indeed been increasingly used by anthropologists when speaking Maya communities outside their homeland (Loucky 1988, 1992; Rodríguez and Hagan 1991; Burns 1993).

2. The 120 municipios located in the western highlands of Guatemala were created by the Spanish colonial state for purposes of state administration of the Maya population (Smith 1984).

3. Pseudonyms are used for the names of all the Maya individuals in the study, as well as for the Guatemalan municipios and settlement areas from which they come. The Department of Totonicapán is an authentic department located in the western highlands of Guatemala. Totonicapán covers an area of roughly one thousand square kilometers and is divided into eight municipios, each of which is identified by its capital town. San Pedro is a pseudonym for one of those eight municipios. The eight municipios are further subdivided into approximately one

thousand smaller farming settlements, referred to as *cantones*, *caseríos*, or *aldeas*.

4. The IRCA legalization program proved more successful than most critics had anticipated, legalizing roughly two-thirds of the estimated eligible population and, in a few places, such as the Southwest, far exceeding preliminary projections (Meissner and Papademetriou 1988; Bean, Edmonston, and Passel 1990a; Hagan and Baker 1993).

👥 CHAPTER FOUR

1. Also provided by IRCA is a series of other legalization programs, including a replenishment agricultural-worker legalization program (RAW), an updated registry program, a program to regularize the status of Cuban and Haitian "entrants," and a program that addresses extended voluntary departure.

2. For a legislative history of IRCA legalization, see Baker 1990, Meissner and Papademetriou 1988, and North and Portz 1989.

3. Legalization, or amnesty, programs have been implemented in several other countries. During the 1970s and early 1980s, Canada, Australia, France, Argentina, and Venezuela all attempted to cope with their migration challenges through temporary legalization programs. The U.S. program, however, stands alone in many ways. Its application period was far longer than other legalization programs—one year, in contrast to a few months in other countries. It involved a complex transition to permanent resident status, whereas most other programs provided a direct transition to permanent residency. Applicants to the United States had to document continual unlawful residence in the United States for more than five years, compared to less than a year in other countries. Also, the U.S. program was the only one to require a hefty application fee. Finally, it legalized roughly 2 million applicants, whereas other programs legalized from 15,000 (Australia) to 30,000 (Venezuela). It was the only pro-

gram of its kind to achieve a turnout approaching preimplementation projections (Baker 1990). The legalization experiences of five other countries are summarized in Meissner, Papademetriou, and North 1986.

4. Houston's was the highest-volume office in the country; however, as a district, it did not approach the numbers filed in Los Angeles, which had sixteen offices to Houston's one.

5. In one innovative study, utilizing a 3:1 ratio of Mexican Americans to Mexican immigrants, Browning and Cullen (1986) estimated the number of undocumented Mexicans in the Houston area to be 100,000. Other studies, which include the recent flow of Central Americans, estimate the undocumented Latino population in Houston to range from 100,000 to 150,000 (Ruggles and Fix 1985; Rodríguez and Hagan 1989).

6. Section 111(c) of IRCA states that the "Attorney General shall provide for improved immigration and naturalization services and for enhanced community outreach and in-service training of personnel. Such enhanced community outreach may include the establishment of appropriate local community task forces to improve the working relationship between the Service [INS] and local community groups and organizations (including employers and organizations representing minorities)." This statutory language drove the development of Houston's Community Task Force.

7. Employer sanctions became effective on December 1, 1986. They were implemented, however, in several phases. The first, which lasted six months, consisted of employer education. In mid-1987, INS began citing employers for violations of the law, but no penalties were imposed. Full enforcement of the sanctions, including penalties, began in June 1988.

👫 **CHAPTER FIVE**

1. Permanent residence through IRCA required the applicant to complete an examination in basic English and civics, or to demonstrate completion of an INS-approved course of instruction.

The Houston public school system as well as private advocacy groups provided these classes, and combined enrollment exceeded twenty thousand students by late 1988 (Baker 1990).

2. Under the 1990 Immigration Act, permanent residents legalized under IRCA have two avenues to petition for visas for spouses and unmarried sons and daughters. Section 111 of the act allocates 114,200 annual, family-sponsored visas for permanent residents. To circumvent a huge backlog under the second-preference category of family-sponsored visas, section 112 of the 1990 act provides an additional 55,000 visas during fiscal years 1992–1994 for the spouses and minor children of eligible legalized aliens. Given that both categories are allocated on a "first come, first serve" basis, we can expect that many of the roughly 3 million people legalized under IRCA (including persons legalized under both the legalization program and the agricultural program) will wait until they become citizens before petitioning for family-sponsored visas, since such a strategy offers immediate immigration to spouses, minor children, as well as parents of U.S. citizens.

3. Six months into the legalization program, the INS revised its regulations, adopting an administrative change that provided derivative protected status to spouses and minor children of legalized persons. Eventually, this "family unity" relief was codified into law as a provision of the 1990 Immigration Act. To be eligible for a temporary stay of deportation and work authorization, however, spouses and children must have entered the United States before May 5, 1988.

🏃 CHAPTER SIX

1. These data are derived from monthly counts of the number of times persons entering the United States without documentation are apprehended by INS or by the U.S. border patrol. There are several problems associated with the use of arrest data to measure undocumented migration. First of all, with these data it is impossible to distinguish the various types of migrants, includ-

ing settlers, sojourners, and commuters (Bean, Vernez, and Keely 1989; Donato, Durand, and Massey 1992). Not only may each of these types have been affected differently by IRCA, but the apprehension data provide no way of distinguishing among them. Secondly, arrest data also include persons who have been apprehended several times, thus overstating the true number of migrants who illegally enter the country over a particular period of time. For example, over 50 percent of the males in the Maya community reported having been apprehended and sent back to Mexico at least once before successfully crossing the U.S.-Mexico border. Moreover, all those who were apprehended identified themselves to the INS as Mexican so that they would be sent back to Mexico rather than Guatemala. If this is a common practice among other Central American groups, it would likewise inflate the figures on Mexican arrests and would deflate those on arrests of persons from Central America. Finally, some persons apprehended in a particular year may return to Mexico or Central America before the end of the year. This, too, tends to overstate the size of the illegal population in any given year. For further discussion of the problematic nature of arrest statistics, see Bean, Vernez, and Keely 1989).

BIBLIOGRAPHY

Adams, Richard N. 1990. "Ethnic Images and Strategies in 1944." In *Guatemalan Indians and the State: 1540–1988*, ed. Carol A. Smith. Austin: University of Texas Press.

Aguayo, Sergio. 1985. *El éxodo centroamericano: Consequencias de un conflicto*. Mexico, D. F.: Secretaría de Educanción Pública (SEP).

Aguayo, Sergio and Patricia Weiss-Fagen. 1988. *Central Americans in Mexico and the United States*. Washington, D.C.: Center for Immigration Policy and Refugee Assistance, Georgetown University.

Alvarez, Lynn and James Loucky. 1992. "Inquiry and Advocacy: Attorney–Expert Collaboration in the Political Asylum Process." In *Anthropologists at Law NAPA Bulletin* 11:43–52.

Americas Watch. 1984. *Guatemalan Refugees in Mexico, 1980–1984*. New York: Americas Watch Committee.

Ayuda, Inc. v. Meese. 1988. 687 F. Supp. 650, 700 F. Supp. 49 (D.D.C.). In *Litigation Alert: Legalization/Special Agricultural Workers*, ed. J. Atkinson. Washington, D.C.: American Immigration Lawyers Association, June 16, 1989.

Baca, R. and D. D. Bryan. 1983. "The 'Assimilation' of Unauthorized Mexican Workers: Another Social Science Fiction?" *Hispanic Journal of Behavioral Science* 5:1–20.

Bach, Robert L. and Howard Brill. 1989. "Shifting the Burden: the Impacts of IRCA on U.S. Labor Markets." Unpublished interim report to the Division of Immigration Policy and Research, U.S. Department of Labor, November.

Bailey, Thomas. 1985. "The Influence of Legal Status on the Labor Market Impact of Immigration." *International Migration Review* 19(2):220–238.

Baker, Susan González. 1990. *The Cautious Welcome: The Legalization Programs of the Immigration Reform and Control Act.* Washington, D.C.: Urban Institute Press.

Balán, Jorge, Harley Browning, and Elizabeth Jelin. 1973. *Men in a Developing Society: Geographic and Social Mobility in Monterrey, Mexico.* Austin: University of Texas Press.

Bean, Frank D., B. Edmonston, and J. Passel, eds. 1990a. *Undocumented Migration to the United States: IRCA and the Experience of the 1980s.* Washington D.C.: Urban Institute Press.

Bean, F. D., T. J. Espenshade, M. J. White, and R. F. Dymowski. 1990b. "Post-IRCA Changes in the Volume and Composition of Undocumented Migration to the United States: An Assessment Based on Apprehensions Data." In *Undocumented Migration to the United States: IRCA and the Experience of the 1980s*, ed. F. D. Bean, B. Edmonston, and J. Passel. Washington, D.C.: Urban Institute Press.

Bean, F. D., A. G. King, and J. S. Passel. 1983. "The Number of Illegal Migrants of Mexican Origin in the United States: Sex Ratio Based Estimates for the 1980s." *Demography* 20:99–109.

Bean, F. D., G. Vernez, and C. B. Keely. 1989. *Opening and Closing the Doors: Evaluating Immigration Reform and Control.* Washington, D.C.: Urban Institute Press.

Beauregard, Robert A. 1989 "Space, Time, and Economic Restructuring." In *Economic Restructuring and Political Response*, ed. Robert A. Beauregard. Newbury Park, Calif.: Sage Publications.

Black, George, Milton Jamail, and Norma Stoltz Chinchilla. 1984. *Garrison Guatemala.* New York: Monthly Review Press.

Borjas, George J. and Marta Tienda. 1994. "The Employment and Wages of Legalized Immigrants." *International Migration Review.* 27(4):712–747.

Boyd, Monica. 1989. "Family and Personal Networks in Migration." *International Migration Review.* 23(3):638–670.

Brintnall, Douglas E. 1979. *Revolt Against the Dead: The Mod-*

ernization of a Mayan Community in the Highlands of Guatemala. New York: Bordon and Breach.

Browning, Harley and Ruth M. Cullen. 1986. "The Complex Demographic Formation of the Mexican-Origin Population." In *Mexican Immigrants and Mexican Americans*, ed. Harley L. Browning and Rodolfo De La Garza. Austin: Center for Mexican American Studies, University of Texas at Austin.

Browning, Harley L. and Nestor Rodríguez. 1985. "The Migration of Mexican Indocumentados as a Settlement Process: Implications for Work." In *Hispanics in the U.S. Economy*, ed. George J. Borjas and Marta Tienda. New York: Academic Press.

Burgos-Debray, Elisabeth, ed. 1984. *I . . . Rigoberta Menchú: An Indian Woman in Guatemala.* New York: Monthly Review Press.

Burns, Allan F. 1988. "Kanjobal Maya Resettlement: Indiantown, Florida." *Cultural Survival Quarterly* 12(4):41–45.

———. 1989. "Internal and External Identity Among Kanjobal Mayan Refugees in Florida." In *Conflict, Migration, and the Expression of Ethnicity*, ed. Gonzalez, Nancy L. and Carolyn S. McCommon. Boulder, Colo.: Westview Press.

———. 1993. *Maya in Exile: Guatemalans in Florida.* Philadelphia: Temple University Press.

Catholic Social Services v. Meese. 1988. No. S-86-1343-LKK (E.D. California, 9th Circuit). In *Litigation Update: Legalization/Special Agricultural Workers*, ed. J. Atkinson. Washington, D.C.: American Immigration Lawyers Association, June 16, 1989.

Chafetz, Janet Saltzman. 1990. *Gender Equity: An Integrated Theory of Stability and Change.* Newbury Park, Calif.: Sage Publications.

Chavez, Leo. 1988. "Settlers and Sojourners: The Case of Mexicans in the United States." *Human Organization* 47:95–108.

———. 1992. *Shadowed Lives: Undocumented Immigrants in American Society.* Orlando: Harcourt Brace Jovanovich.

Cornelius, Wayne A. 1982. "Interviewing Undocumented Immigrants: Methodological Reflections Based on Fieldwork in Mexico and the U.S." *Working papers in U.S.-Mexican Studies*, 2. San Diego: Program in United States-Mexican Studies, University of California.

———. 1989. "Impacts of the 1986 U.S. Immigration Law on Emigration from Rural Mexican Sending Communities." *Population and Development Review* 15:689–705.

Cornelius, Wayne A. and Phillip Martin 1993. "The Uncertain Connection: Free Trade and Rural Mexican Migration to the United States." *International Migration Review* 27(3):484–512.

Cross, H.G., J. Mell Kenney, and W. Zimmerman. 1990. *Employer Hiring Practices: Differential Treatment of Hispanic and Anglo Job Seekers*. Washington, D.C.: Urban Institute Press.

Dalli Sante, Angela. 1983. "Crisis in Guatemala: Repression, Refugees, and Responsibilities." *Our Socialism* 1(5):1–30.

DGE, (Dirección General de Estadística). 1968. *Censos nacionales: IV Habitación–IX Población*. Guatemala City: República de Guatemala, Ministerio de Economía.

———. 1984. *Censos nacionales: IV Habitación–IX Población*. Guatemala City: República de Guatemala, Ministerio de Economía.

Donato, K. M., J. Durand, and D. S. Massey. 1992. "Stemming the Tide? Assessing the Deterrent Effects of the Immigration Reform and Control Act." *Demography* 29(2):141–157.

Donato, K. M. and D. S. Massey. 1993. "Effect of the Immigration Reform and Control Act on the Wages of Mexican Migrants." *Social Science Quarterly*. 74(3):523–541.

Feagin, Joe R. 1988. *Free Enterprise City: Houston in Political and Economic Perspective*. New Brunswick, N.J.: Rutgers University Press.

Ferris, Elizabeth G. 1987. *The Central American Refugees*. New York: Praeger Publishers.

Frelick, William. 1991. *Running the Gauntlet: The Central American Journey Through Mexico*. Washington, D.C.: U.S. Committee for Refugees.

Fuentes, Annette. 1988. "Immigration Reform: Heaviest Burden on Women." *Listen Real Loud*. Philadelphia: American Friends Service Committee.

González de la Rocha, M. and A. Escobar Latapí. 1990. "The Impact of IRCA on the Migration Patterns on a Community in Los Altos, Jalisco, Mexico." In *Unauthorized Migration: Addressing the Root Causes*. Research Addendum, Supplement. Washington, D.C.: Commission for the Study of International Migration and Cooperative Economic Development.

Granovetter, Mark S. 1973. "The Strength of Weak Ties." *American Journal of Sociology* 78(6):1360–1380.

Grasmuck, Sherri 1984. "Immigration, Ethnic Stratification and Native Working-Class Discipline: Comparisons of Documented Dominicans." *International Migration Review* 18(3):692–713.

Grasmuck, Sherri and Patricia Pessar. 1991. *Between Two Islands: Dominican International Migration*. Berkeley: University of California Press.

Hagan, Jacqueline M. 1986. "The Politics of Numbers: Central American Migration During a Period of Crisis, 1978–1985." Master's thesis, University of Texas at Austin.

———. 1989. "Interim Report on the Effects of IRCA on Houston's Domestic Industry." Unpublished paper.

Hagan, Jacqueline M. and Susan González Baker. 1993. "Implementing the U.S. Legalization Program: The Influence of Immigrant Communities and Local Agencies on Immigration Policy Reform." *International Migration Review* 27(3):513–536.

Hagan, Jacqueline M. and Nestor P. Rodríguez. 1992. "Recent Economic Restructuring and Evolving Intergroup Relations in Houston." In *Structuring Diversity: Ethnographic Perspectives on the New Immigration*, ed. Louise Lamphere. Chicago: University of Chicago Press.

Henderson, Jeffrey and Manuel Castells. 1987. *Global Restructuring and Territorial Development*. London: Sage Publications.

Hiracheta v. Thornburgh. 1989. CA3-89-1161-F (N.D. Texas). In *Litigation Update: Legalization/Special Agricultural Workers*, ed. J. Atkinson. Washington, D.C.: American Immigration Lawyers Association, June 16, 1989.

Hondagneu-Sotelo, Perrette. 1992. "Overcoming Patriarchal Constraints: The Reconstruction of Gender Relations Among Mexican Immigrant Women and Men." *Gender and Society* 6(3):393–445.

Houston Chronicle. 1988. May 1, October 29, and November 7.

INS (Immigration and Naturalization Service), U.S. Department of Justice. 1992. *Immigration and Control Act: Report on the Legalized Population*. Washington, D.C.: U.S. Government Printing Office, March.

Keely, Charles ·B. 1989. "Population and Immigration Policy: State and Federal Roles." In *Mexican and Central American Population and the U.S.* Immigration Policy, ed. F. D. Bean, J. Schmandt, and S. Weintraub. Austin: University of Texas Press.

Kluck, P. A. 1983. "The Society and its Environment." In *Guatemala: A Country Study*, ed. Richard F. Nyrop. Washington, D.C.: Foreign Area Studies, the American University.

Kritz, Mary and Douglas T. Gurak. 1984. "Kinship Assistance in the Settlement Process: Dominican and Colombian Cases." Paper presented at the annual meeting of the Population Association of America, Minneapolis, Minn., May.

Loe v. Thornburgh. 1989. No. 88 Civ. 7363 (PKL) (S.D. New York). In *Litigation Update: Legalization/Special Agricultural Workers*, ed. J. Atkinson. Washington, D.C.: American Immigration Lawyers Association, June 16, 1989.

Lomnitz, Larissa. 1977. *Networks and Marginality: Life in a Mexican Shantytown*. New York: Academic Press.

Loucky, James. 1988. "Rejection, Reaffirmation, or Redefinition: Changing Identity of Indigenous Guatemalans in Los Angeles." Paper presented at annual meeting of the American Anthropological Association, November 17, 1988.

———. 1992. "Central American Refugees: Learning New Skills

in the U.S.A." In *Anthropology: Understanding Human Adaptation*, ed. Michael C. Howard and Janet Dunaif-Hattis. New York: HarperCollins.

Loucky, James and Norma Chinchilla. 1989. "The Effects of IRCA on Selected Industries in Los Angeles: A Preliminary Report." Unpublished paper.

Lowell, B. L., D. A. Cobb-Clark, C. Shiells, and E. Haghighat. 1991. "IRCA and Metropolitan Labor Markets: Disentangling the Effects of Employer Sanctions and Legalization." Paper presented at the meeting of the American Sociological Association, Cincinnati, August 23–27, 1991.

Macdonald, John S. and Leatrice D. Macdonald. 1974. "Chain Migration, Ethnic Neighborhood Formation, and Social Networks." In *An Urban World*, ed. Charles Tilly. Boston: Little, Brown.

Manz, Beatriz. 1988. *Refugees of Hidden War: The Aftermath of Counterinsurgency in Guatemala*. Albany: State University of New York Press.

Massey, Douglas S. 1987a. "Understanding Mexican Migration to the United States." *American Journal of Sociology* 92:1372–1403.

———. 1987b. "Do Undocumented Immigrants Earn Lower Wages than Legal Immigrants? New Evidence from Mexico." *International Migration Review* 21(2) 733–738.

Massey, Douglas, Rafael Alarcon, Jorge Durand, and Humberto González. 1987. *Return to Aztlan: The Social Process of Migration from Western Mexico*. Berkeley: University of California Press.

Massey, Douglas S., K. M. Donato, and Z. Liang. 1990. "Effects of the Immigration Reform and Control Act of 1986: Preliminary Data from Mexico." In *Undocumented Migration to the United States: IRCA and the Experience of the 1980s*, ed. F. D. Bean, B. Edmonston, and J. Passel. Washington, D.C.: Urban Institute Press.

McBryde, Felix Webster. 1945. *Cultural and Historical Geography of Southwest Guatemala*. Publication no. 4. Washington,

D.C.: Institute of Social Anthropology, Smithsonian Institution.

Meissner, D. and D. Papademetriou. 1988. *The Legalization Countdown: A Third-Quarter Assessment*. Washington, D.C.: Carnegie Endowment for International Peace.

Meissner, D., D. Papademetriou, and D. North. 1986. *Legalization of Undocumented Aliens: Lessons from Other Countries*. Washington, D.C.: Carnegie Endowment for International Peace.

Melville, M. B. 1978. "Mexican Women Adapt to Migration." *International Migration Review* 12(2):225–235.

Miller, Harris N. 1985. "The Right Thing to Do: A History of Simpson-Mazzoli." In *Clamor at the Gates: The New American Immigration*, ed. Nathan Glazer. San Francisco: Institute for Contemporary Studies Press.

Miralles, Maria. 1986. "Health Seeking Behaviors of Guatemalan Refugees in South Florida." Master's thesis, University of Florida, Gainsville.

Nash, Manning. 1967. *Machine Age Maya: Industrialization of a Guatemalan Community*. Chicago: University of Chicago Press.

North, David S. and Mary Ann Portz. 1989. *The U.S. Legalization Program*. Washington D.C.: TransCentury Development Associates.

Pensola, F. 1986. *Central Americans In Los Angeles: Background, Language, Education*. Occasional Paper no. 21. Los Angeles: Spanish-Speaking Mental Health Research Center.

Pessar, Patricia R. 1982. "The Role of Households in International Migration and the Case of U.S.-Bound Migration from the Dominican Republic." *International Migration Review* 16(2):342–364.

———. 1986. "The Role of Gender in Dominican Settlement in the United States." In *Women and Change in Latin America*, ed. June Nash and Helen Safa. South Hadley, Mass.: Bergin and Garvey.

Pinkerton, James. 1993. "Border Patrol Plans to Fence Out Mexico." *Houston Chronicle*, December 11.

Piper, R. P. and A. Reynolds. 1991. *The Path to North American Economic Integration: Lessons from the European Community's Experience*. Indianapolis: Hudson Institute.

Portes, Alejandro and Robert L. Bach. 1985. *Latin Journey: Cuban and Mexican Immigrants in the United States*. Berkeley: University of California Press.

Portes, Alejandro and John W. Curtis. 1987. "Changing Flags: Naturalization and its Determinants among Mexican Immigrants. *International Migration Review* 21(2):352–372.

Portes, Alejandro and Cynthia Truelove. 1987. "Making Sense of Diversity: Recent Research on Hispanic Minorities in the United States." *Annual Review of Sociology* 13:359–385.

Redfield, Robert. 1934. "Folk Ways and City Ways." In *Human Nature and the Study of Society: The Papers of Robert Redfield*, vol. 1, ed. M. P. Redfield. Chicago: University of Chicago Press.

Reina, Rubén E. 1957. "Chinautla: A Guatemalan Indian Community." Ph.D. diss., University of North Carolina.

Repak, Terry A. 1989. "The Impact of Employer Sanctions on the Construction and Domestic Industries in Washington, D.C." Unpublished paper.

———. 1994. "Labor Market Incorporation of Central American Immigrants in Washington, D.C." *Social Problems* 41(1):114–128.

REVAC (Real Estate Evaluation Consultants). 1990. *Harris County Apartment Occupancy and Rental Survey*. Houston REVAC.

Roberts, Bryan R. 1974. "The Interrelations of Cities and Provinces in Peru and Guatemala." In *Latin American Urban Research IV*, ed. Wayne A. Cornelius and Felicity M. Trueblood. Beverly Hills and London: Sage Publications.

Rodríguez, Nestor P. 1987. "Undocumented Central Americans in Houston: Diverse Populations." *International Migration Review* 21(1):4–25.

————. 1989a. "Undocumented Mayan Migration to the United States: Findings in a Sending Community." Paper presented at the American Sociological Association meeting, San Francisco, August 9–13.

————. 1989b. "Interim Report on the Effects of IRCA in Houston." Unpublished paper.

Rodríguez, Nestor P. and Jacqueline M. Hagan. 1989. "Undocumented Central American Migration to Houston in the 1980s." *Journal of La Raza Studies* 2(1):1–4.

————. 1991. "Investigating Census Coverage and Content Among the Undocumented: An Ethnographic Study of Latino Tenants in Houston." In *Ethnographic Evaluation of the 1990 Decennial Census Report Series*. Report 3. Washington, D.C.: Center for Survey Research Methods, U.S. Bureau of the Census.

————. 1992. "Apartment Restructuring and Latino Immigrant Tenant Struggles: A Case Study of Human Agency." *Comparative Urban and Community Research* 4:164–180.

Rosen, Pat. 1990. "City Apartment Demolitions Picking Up after a Slow Start." *Houston Business Journal*, October, 1.

Ruggles, P. and M. Fix. 1985. *Impacts and Potential Impacts of Central American Migrants on Health and Human Services and Related Programs of Assistance*. Washington, D.C.: Urban Institute Press.

Sallee, Rad. 1991. "Minorities Now Majority in Houston." *Houston Chronicle*, February 8.

SCIRP (Select Commission on Immigration and Refugee Policy). 1981. *U.S. Immigration Policy and the National Interest: The Staff Report of the Select Commission on Immigration Policy*. Washington, D.C.: U.S. Government Printing Office. March 1.

Shelton, Beth Ann, Nestor P. Rodríguez, Joe R. Feagin, Robert D. Bullard, and Robert D. Thomas. 1989. *Houston: Growth and Decline in a Sunbelt Boomtown*. Philadelphia: Temple University Press.

Simon Rita, J. and Caroline B. Brettell. 1986. *International*

Migration: The Female Experience. Totowa, N.J.: Rowman & Allanheld.

Smith, Carol A. 1984. "Does a Commodity Economy Enrich the Few While Ruining the Masses?: Differentiation among Petty Commodity Producers in Guatemala." *Journal of Peasant Studies* 11:60–95.

———. 1988. "Destruction of the Material Bases for Indian Culture." In *Harvest of Violence: The Mayan Indians and the Guatemalan Crisis*, ed. Robert Carmack. Norman: University of Oklahoma Press.

———. 1989. "Survival Strategies among Petty Commodity Producers." *International Labour Review* 128:791–813.

———. 1990. "Introduction: Social Relations in Guatemala Over Time and Space." In *Guatemalan Indians and the State: 1540–1988*, ed. Carol A. Smith. Austin: University of Texas Press.

Tax, Sol. 1937. "The Municipios of the Midwestern Highlands of Guatemala." *American Anthropologist* 39(3):423–444.

Tienda, Marta and Karen Booth. 1991. "Gender, Migration, and Social Change." *International Sociology* 6:51–72.

Tienda, Marta and Audrey Singer. Forthcoming. "The Wage Mobility of Undocumented Workers in the United States." *International Migration Review*.

Tilly, Charles and Harold Brown. 1967. "On Uprooting, Kinship, and the Auspices of Migration." *International Journal of Comparative Sociology*. 8:139–164.

Torres-Rivas, Edelberto. 1985. *Report on the Conditions of Central American Refugees and Migrants*. Hemispheric Migration Project, Occasional Paper Series. Washington, D.C.: Center for Immigration Policy and Refugee Assistance, Georgetown University.

U.S. Department of Commerce, Bureau of the Census. 1991. *1990 Census of Population and Housing: Summary of Population and Housing Characteristics, Texas*. 1990 CPH-1-45, table 3. Washington D.C.: Government Printing Office.

U.S. General Accounting Office. 1987. *Immigration Reform: Status of Implementing Employer Sanctions After One Year.* GAO/GGD-88-14, November 5. Washington, D.C.: Government Printing Office.

———. 1988. *Immigration Reform: Status of Implementing Employer Sanctions After Second Year.* GAO/GGD-89-16, November 15. Washington, D.C.: Government Printing Office.

———. 1990. *Immigration Reform: Employer Sanctions and the Question of Discrimination.* GAO/GGD-90-62, March 29. Washington, D.C.: Government Printing Office.

U.S. House of Representatives. 1986. *Immigration Control and Legalization Amendments Act of 1986.* Judiciary Committee Report 99-682. 99th Congress, 2nd session. July 16.

Veblen, Thomas T. 1982. "Native Population Decline in Totonicapán, Guatemala." In *The Historical Demography of Highland Guatemala*, eds. Robert M. Carmack, John Early, and Christopher Lutz. Albany: Institute for Mesoamerican Studies, State University of New York at Albany.

Vialet, Joyce C. and Larry M. Eig. 1990. *Immigration Act of 1990 (P.L. 101–649).* Washington, D.C.: Congressional Research Service.

Wagley, Charles. 1941. *Economics of a Guatemalan Village.* Memoirs of the American Anthropological Association no. 58. Menasha, Wisc.: American Anthropological Association.

———. 1949. *The Social and Religious Life of a Guatemala Village.* Memoirs of the American Anthropological Association, no. 71. Menasha, Wisc.: American Anthropological Association.

Warren, Kay B. 1978. *The Symbolism of Subordination: Indian Identity in a Guatemalan Town.* Austin: University of Texas Press.

Watanabe, John M. 1984. *"We Who Are Here": The Cultural Conventions of Ethnic Identity in a Guatemalan Indian Village, 1937–1980.* Ph.D. diss. Harvard University. Ann Arbor, Mich.: University Microfilms.

———. 1990. "Enduring Yet Ineffable Community in the Western Periphery of Guatemala. In *Guatemalan Indians and the State: 1540–1988*, ed. Carol A. Smith. Austin: University of Texas Press.

Zambrano v. Meese. 1988. No. S-88-455-EJG-M (E.D. California). In *Litigation Update: Legalization/Special Agricultural Workers*. ed. J. Atkinson. Washington, D.C.: American Immigration Lawyers Association. June 16, 1989:3.

INDEX